Alone WITH GOD

The Rose of Sharon

BARBARA RENEÉ JOHNSON

Alone with God
The Rose of Sharon
by Barbara Reneé Johnson

Printed in the United States of America

ISBN 9781629523118

Unless otherwise indicated, Bible quotations are taken from English Standard Version. Copyright © 1971 by Crossway Bibles, a division of Good News Publishers.

www.xulonpress.com

ACKNOWLEDGEMENTS

In all of thy ways acknowledge Him and He shall direct your path. (Prov. 3:6) I am thankful to the Lord for giving me the strength to maximize my potential.

I honor the memory of my parents, the late James B. Hicks, and the late Patricia Buggs. I will forever be grateful for the sacrifices and parental guidance of my grandmother, Verdie B. Nelson, who raised me. To my husband, Pastor Vernon B. Johnson, thank you for your love and continued support. To my four sons: Marquintez, Demetrius, Melchisedec, and Isaiah Johnson, greater works shall you do. I love you dearly!

To my co-workers and clients from the beauty salons in the United States and abroad, thank you for your prayers and support. I appreciate the members of Culpepper Christian Servicemen Center for their love and support. Special thanks to the Intercessory prayer team. Your prayers have made this book possible.

I am thankful to the Hicks, Henry, and Boone family. To the United States Army Garrison Community and friends, thanks you for believing in my dream. Thanks to Bob and Patti Moore, Directors of The Far East Christian Servicemen's Centers, for your prayers and support.

I would like to express my gratitude to the Spring Hill Baptist Church of Oakland, Louisiana, and Pastor Baker of the First Apostolic Church of El Dorado, Arkansas, for providing a platform for me to share the gospel during my visits while in the states.

Many thanks to the following: The pastors and prophets who obeyed God and for speaking in my life; Pastor Lennie & Christine Clemons of Wesson Street Church of God in Christ (El Dorado, Arkansas); Pastor Williams of The Greater North Church of God in Christ Garlstedt, Germany); Bishop C.E. & Marcia Harris of Emmanuel Temple (Wahiawa, Hawaii); The late Rev C.H. Foy of The Mount Carmel Baptist Church (Houston, Texas); Pastors Annette & Randy Thomas (Lawton, Oklahoma); and Pastor John & Zula Green and the Culpepper Christian Servicemen Center (Seoul, Korea).

To God be the glory for things He has done, and for what He shall do!

Barbara Renea Johnson

TABLE OF CONTENTS

MY STORY BEGINS

 $\mathscr{I}$ was born in Eldorado, Arkansas on February 16, 1969 to James B. Hicks of Strong, Arkansas and Patricia Nelson of Eldorado, Arkansas. One year and two months after I was born, my father was killed in the Vietnam War.

I was blessed to meet Vernon Johnson in my sophomore year of high school. He was convinced that God sent him to rescue me. He was persistent and we were married two weeks after my graduation from Eldorado High School. We have weathered many storms, but remain together. We have four sons: Marquintez, Demetrius, Melchisedec, and Isaiah Johnson. They are world changers for the Kingdom of God.

As an only child, I took advantage of many opportunities to be alone with God. I did not have the privilege of knowing my father, nor did I have a male figure in my home. Thus I accepted Jesus as my Father at a young age.

My mother, whom I called Pat, gave birth to me when she was very young. She chose not to be a mother and gave me to my maternal grandmother, Verdie B. Nelson, to raise me. Pat was like the sister I had never had. I loved and respected her regardless of the choices she made and the affect her choices made on my life. She would constantly say to me: "Don't be like me, be better!"

Pat was adventurous and searched for love in the wrong places and from the wrong people. Although she and my father were never married, I have always wondered if his death led to her troubled life as an alcoholic and a drug addict. She trusted men with no character and followed them across the country. She eventually got married, and later, divorced. I always prayed that God would keep her safe and that she would eventually settle down and maintain consistent communication with me.

I stayed in contact with Pat as much as I could by calling her and asking my grandmother about her. Because I saw the pain and agony she was experiencing trying to maintain her own life, I never resented her for not raising me. She was always in my prayers, but I never prayed to be under her guidance. She lived a wayward life during most of my school years, but began to make wiser choices during my senior year of high school. Her life changed for the better, and so did our communications. Our relationship blossomed. Pat began babysitting children in the community. Interestingly enough, while she did not raise me, she was drawn to these children. It was commonly known in the community of her love and care for the youth.

Pat got remarried and even though the marriage started off rocky, she and her husband reconciled their differences and remained together. She was readily available to me for the next four years, until I relocated to Germany with my husband, who was in the military. When I gave birth to my first son, Pat vowed to be the best grandmother anyone could imagine. After I returned from Germany she started babysitting my children. She and my grandmother would often pitch in and buy gifts for my children during the holidays.

On December 15, 2000, my mother was hospitalized in Eldorado, Arkansas for a minor procedure. At that time, I resided in Lawton, Oklahoma, so I traveled to be with her. During my visit with Pat in the hospital, she suggested I get paper and pen and write down what she wanted me to know. She made her own funeral arrangements, shared with me the names of people she wanted to appear on the program, and described where she wanted to be buried. She told me that she was very proud of me and expressed her regrets for not being a better mother to me. I was surprised by what I was hearing, but embraced her words.

Pat was released from the hospital with a favorable report and was expected to recover speedily. Two months later, on February 17, 2001, I received news that my mother died of a heart attack while taking a bath. I believe my mother knew that her time on earth was coming to an end. I was left alone to carry out her desires. I went shopping for the dress my mother requested and fixed her hair. I presented her obituary exactly as she wanted it.

Back to my grandmother, the woman who raised me. My grandmother had a third grade education. She worked cleaning homes and cooking in restaurants. There were times when we did not have electricity, water, or gas. When she could not afford to pay the water bill we would carry water from a neighbor so we could take a bath, wash our clothes, and flush the toilet. When we did not have electricity, we completed certain tasks before dark. During the winter we covered the windows with plastic to keep an already cold house from getting colder.

I mostly washed my clothes by hand and used a neighbor's clothesline to hang my garments to dry. Occasionally, there was extra money and I was dropped off at the laundromat to do my laundry. There were days I went to school wearing clothes that were still wet. We ate food that my grandmother brought home from the private homes of her employers. I did not have many friends, because I did not want my peers to know about my living conditions. We did not own a vehicle until my sophomore year in high school and all of our furniture was used or given to us by others.

My childhood was filled with many obstacles and challenges. Poverty was my normal. My great-grandmother, my grandmother's mother, Selma Henry, started taking me to church. I accepted Jesus as my Savior at age nine. The Lord became real to me and filled all of my voids. I looked forward to going to church. After I got home from church, I would sing all of the songs, rehearse the sermons, and practice my hallelujah dance. I would tell God how much I loved Him and thanked Him for blessing me with my mother, my Uncle Will, and my grandmother, in spite of my living conditions.

I am grateful to God for giving me to my grandmother and for giving her to me. After Pat's death, I was blessed to be able to relocate my grandmother. She lived with my family in Oklahoma for four years. My husband received orders from the military to go to Seoul, Korea. Due to her health, my grandmother was not able to travel. For several years, she resided in a nursing home in Eldorado, Arkansas where my phone calls to her were daily and extended visits were constant.

On March 29, 2014, just two days before my first book, Alone with God, was to be published, with me at her bedside. My grandmother went home to be with the Lord. She had dedicated her life to the Lord in 2005, so I am at peace knowing that heaven is her eternal home, but how I miss her! She was my gift from God! She was not able to give me elegant things in life, but her wisdom and love helped shape my life and is leading me to my destiny.

INTRODUCTION

*A*lmost everyone has experienced loneliness at some point in their lives. Whether it was cause by personal choices, relocation, life challenges, or the loss of love one. Some people don't realize that loneliness can be as deadly as a chronic disease. There are millions of people who suffer from loneliness, the silent killer. To fill the void of loneliness, perhaps you have tried social media or revolving relationships. Maybe you have accumulated wealth or even developed habits that have become addictive.

If nothing has worked for you, perhaps this book will give you applications that can make you content being alone with God, but no longer experiencing loneliness. I wrote this book to share my challenges of being an only child and the obstacles I faced growing up in poverty. Some benefits from reading this book could be developing a closer spiritual relationship with God and utilizing applications that will make you feel surrounded by the love of God. It will help you use adversities and limitations as opportunities to propel you to meet your destiny.

My goal is to plant seeds of victory in your life. The lyrics of my struggles have been shared in many conferences, retreats, revivals, and prophetic rallies around the world. This book is certainly Bible orchestrated. It can easily be used in your daily life as a devotion and teaching guide with engaging personal testimony. You will love the unique approach toward my personal relationship with God.

Each chapter will lift your spirit and develop an urgency to be closer to God. It will unveil the mysteries of identity and release true acceptance. Being alone with God is the best way to know his voice and embrace his presence. There are many seats in an average vehicle but there is only one steering wheel. Allow God to be the driving force in your life, and He will allow you to arrive at your destination on schedule.

God is always extending invitations for fellowship, friendship, and most of all, a relationship. His requirements are for those who come to accept Him and His standards. There is no need to bring money, food, or render your expertise, but come with a desire to be complete in Him. God longs to be alone with us and it will only cost us time and honesty. Most of all, being alone with God takes away all your loneliness!

Chapter 1

DESPERATE FOR THE PRESENCE OF GOD

*H*ave you ever experienced a mighty move of God during your worship service? Maybe there was a gospel song you heard and the lyrics described your current pain. It soothed your brokenness and you played the song over and over again. We all have seen the presence of God moving in someone during church service. They just couldn't seem to stop praising God by clapping their hands, crying, screaming, or maybe even jumping and shouting. God's presence is so amazing and it seems as though we can never get enough or don't want it to ever end. Some people desire the ability to just wrap it up and put in a box, granting the privilege to open and close it freely. Unfortunately, it is not that easy. Those desiring to feel the presence of God must have the attitude of "by any means necessary". We must allow Him to have authority and access by creating a welcoming atmosphere that meets His standards. God can arrive without notice when our pursuit for Him is pure.

In order to place a demand on the Holy Spirit, we must be willing to have a lifestyle of prayer, eagerness to learn, and the humility to change. With today's fast-paced way of living, many things are going on around us that can be distractions. We can get lost in the shuffle, mishandle our priorities, lose our foundation, and put the things of God last. Convenience becomes our first choice. We give God limited time and space, which is what I call "the leftovers". In order to be desperate for God, a sacrifice must be rendered. It is time to stand against all odds and be willing to forsake all others.

Let's take a look at what happen when a few people from the Bible made sacrifices to God. Abraham was willing to sacrifice his son and found the ram in the bush. His faith was increased knowing that God would do just as he promised. Abigail sacrificed her life (while not aware of how David and his army would receive her) and interceded for her husband Nabal. God spared her life and prevented the king from shedding innocent blood. Hannah vowed to have her son be raised by the king. She sacrificed her motherhood to honor God for blessing her womb. The woman with an alabaster box sacrificed the profit from the oil. She was made famous for crowning Jesus as king before the crucifixion. Gideon sacrificed a reduction of his army. God revealed that victory is not in the numbers but with those that will hear, obey his voice, and be in accord with the will of our father!

Selfless services and sacrifices simply mean surrendering and submitting anything of value for a remarkable outcome. Throughout my experience of purchasing items, I was not always able to instantly buy what I wanted. Sometimes I had to wait, prioritize need versus want, or just not buy the item. Making a sacrifice is somewhat like collateral that is used for a valuable investment such as a down payment, installment plan, or lay-away. God observes the sacrifice to determine His investments and the value of our blessings. Jesus mentioned on the cross that His desire was to please the father and suffer for the sins of the world, knowing that it would be worth the self-denial.

In Luke 9:23 (KJV), Jesus said unto them: "If any man will come after me let him deny himself, and take up his cross daily, and follow me." Many Christians expect God to respond under their personal conditions, timing, and methods. At the beginning of year, we believe and we confess that God's going to do a new thing. However, many Christians do not understand the concept of old and new. In order to get the new, we must release the old. Yes, that's right, give up to get in. God constantly reminds us as his followers that extravagant exchanges will increase our faith. God Himself gave his only begotten son so those who choose Him can have eternal life.

This passage of scripture is extending an invitation to everyone. Come, share your loneliness, burdens, and troubles. The investment in the kingdom does not go unnoticed or unpaid. "To all who mourn in Israel, he will give a crown of beauty for ashes, a joyous blessing instead of mourning, festive praise instead of despair. In their righteousness, they will be like great oaks that the LORD has planted for his own glory." (Isa. 61:3 NIV)

There is an amazing transformation that takes place with spoken confessions. The heart can be converted, which changes the mindset and lifestyle. The world is full of negative influence and opportunities to be misled. The negative influence persuades some people to believe they can gain everything without endurance. Some people become misled and debate with the word of God.

Isaiah 1:18-19 (NIV) states: "Come now and let us reason together, said the Lord; though your sins be as scarlet, they will be as white as snow; though they be red like crimson, they will be as wool. If you are willing and obedient, you shall eat the good of the land;"

Only God can manifest these changes. He reminds us in Matthew 9: 16-17 (KJV): "No man can putteth a piece of new cloth unto an old garment, for that which is put in to fill it up taketh from the garment, and the rent is made worse. Neither do men put new wine into old bottles: else the bottles break, and the wine runneth out, and the bottles perish: but they put new wine into new bottles, and both are preserved." Technology has changed over the years and none of the old methods seem to be as efficient today. We tend to focus on space preservation, speed, and easier access. Old equipment will not fit or work with technical advancements. Our Christian progression is almost the same.

Fifty percent of people become relaxed because of past victories and don't realize that there are more battles to overcome. It is better not to negotiate or rationalize with people and things. Recognize that past challenges were considered as spiritual boot camp toward success. Failures and disappointments along with other challenges in life become building blocks to establish a foundation toward a brighter future. Don't misunderstand me by insinuating I am recommending you end a marriage or get rid of an antique possession; both can become more valuable with time than any other possession. Satan, our opponent, uses a strategy to make Christians believe one can continue to satisfy his or her own desires and please people while still maintaining truth and purity. Not so! When Christians refuse to surrender all to God, it gives space for negativity to gain ground and rule.

This is one of the many reasons we should not rely on our own intellect, but seek wise Godly counsel about our decisions. Those who bargain to eliminate the process diminish the strength of the foundation. I heard people say, "I don't do the things I use to, I don't go the places I use to go, and I don't talk the way I use to talk." But are we doing any maintenance towards enhancing our relationship with God? Our journeys as believers are continuously growing which position us for greater challenges as well as blessings. These are a few questions I would like us to ponder. Do we know the voice of God? Is there an excitement to please him? How many souls have we introduced to Christ within the last three months? We should encourage others to get in the place of God and not support or engage in negative conversations that divide the kingdom.

We should be willing to give time in prayer and presenting our bodies as a living sacrifice as we intercede for others. Do you have a personal alter? This is the place that you should design in your home and reserve it to be the place to put your flesh (your will and your way) under subjection. Repent and become pure to get in God's presence. The altar can be considered a monumental place. Yes, put all of your negative thoughts and your selfish wills in the Tomb of forgetfulness. We must disconnect ourselves from sin that separate us from God. Give up the limitation of God only moving in a Church environment. The glory of God can appear anywhere the atmosphere is set. Each chapter in this book will end with a section called "Place of Communion" It consist of a prayer that acknowledges God, confession of sin, commitment of improvement, and thanksgiving. Applications are listed to guide us along our Christian journey. I believe it will enrich our relationship with God and others.

Ecclesiastes 1:9 reminds us: "The thing that hath been, it is that which shall be; and that which is done is that which shall be done; and there is no new thing under the sun."

My grandmother would tell me, "God never changes, but people do." We must get in the place that God has created for his people. There is nothing new under the sun but it becomes new when we embrace God's way instead of the way we want it, or the way it's been done in the past. There is a standard in God we must reach before we can have the abundance of peace and contentment. Obedience to God will enable us to receive what is new to us as a fulfillment from God. There is a first time for everything and that's a portion of what makes it new!

Philippians 3:14-15 states: "Brethren, I count not myself to have apprehended; but this one thing I do forgetting those things which are behind, and reaching forth unto those things which are before. I press toward the mark for the prize of the high calling of God in Christ Jesus. Let us therefore, as many as be perfect, be thus minded; and if anything be otherwise minded, God shall reveal even this unto you."

We still have unanswered prayers that God will have a season for answering. There is a wealthy place in our lives that has not reached its highest capacity. There are children that are yet been born. There are women and men who are left to make a covenant in marriage. There are books not yet published. There are more songs that haven't been written. There are melodies of music that haven't been played. There are sermons that haven't been preached. There are sicknesses that have not been healed. There are lessons to be learned and subjects to be taught. There is land that hasn't been purchased. There are houses that haven't been built. There are many blessing we can still receive. There are promises that are yet to be fulfilled. There are job vacancies reserved for employment. There are promotions that have not been given. There is a seed time and a harvest time. We still have seeds to sow, people to meet, gifts to be stirred, and places we must go. Now you ought to give God praise for yours. This is not about a church building but a living individual body (the Church).

There are many opportunities for goals and dreams to be accomplished. Nevertheless we must take ownership. We must realize that God has a place that is tailor made and reserved for everyone. We must not lean to our own understanding (Prov. 3:5)

Listen, give up Satan's playground (works of the flesh) and worldly influences and let's get in the presence of God. We can do all things through Christ that strengthen us. (Phil. 4:13) We must be sober and valiant and must analyze our motives and methods. (1 Peter 5:8) Do a self-observation. The first question should be, "Do my works enlarge the kingdom or are they my selfish ambitions?" Don't be deceived! Positions and titles do not impress God.

Let's take a closer look at where the opponent (Satan) lurks. Psalms17:12 and Psalms 91:1-2 reminds us He that dwelt in the secret place of the most high shall abide under the shadow of the Almighty. If we don't abide in God with our whole heart and live a Holy lifestyle, we become an open target to our opponent.

Our opponent (Satan) is always in the recruiting business. He targets those who are not exercising their faith in God. He aims at those who don't really know the word of God for themselves.

He also seeks the weak and feeble. Sometimes with the hustle and bustle we tend to get too busy. We focus more on the work of the ministries than the ministry itself. In accordance with Matthew 7:22-23, let's begin the process by good old fashion repentance at the altar. Confess all our sins and shortcomings to God to include refusal to forgive others, bitterness, and anything that separates us from God.

The alarm has sounded off and there is no time for excuses. (John 5:7) There is no reason to depend on the praise and worship to sing you into presence of God. There is no need to wait on ministers to preach you free. There is no need to wait or (pay) a prophet to speak the word into your life.

I could have easily played the blame game with God for taking my father. I could have chosen to live in bitterness toward my mother for childhood incongruity but I learned to take one day at a time. God knows the fundamental maturity of his investment. He knows exactly what it takes for me to choose him completely. I became desperate for Him at an early age because I heard that he would never leave me. I found myself talking to Him about things I wanted to share with my natural father. He has proved to be my heavenly father here on earth. I would talk to God about my mother and things I desired us to do together. God filled the absence of my parents by placing the right people around me. I knew with God I could be safe, secure, and satisfied. I started to believe every word spoken from the Bible. God's word became my anchor and it kept me focused. I believed that a brighter day was coming my way. I learned to accept my current condition, and I realized that it does not dictate who I am as a person. I am a child of the highest King. I believe that my best days are ahead. My future is greater than my past and so is yours.

There is no need to procrastinate on being in God's presence. He has made all necessary arrangements for everyone to be invited. On the day of Jesus Christ's crucifixion the curtain in the temple were torn from top to bottom. Before the sacrifice of Jesus, there were ceremonies of animal sacrifices. The sacrifices were once year atonements for the sin of men. Only the priests were allowed to go beyond the veil. Jesus Christ is the perfect sacrifice for all mankind sins for now and forever. Now we can speak to God on our behalf and enter into HIS gates with thanksgiving and into courts with praise. Accept Jesus into your hear. Believe that He died for our sins and confess your sins to Him. He will never leave or forsake you. Nothing can ever separate us from God, except our sin. Our acknowledgements of him always allow us to be in his presence. God has eliminated all barriers that would keep us from coming to him. Accept his personal invitation and come where the table is spread and the feast of the Lord is going on. Ephesians 5:19 tells us: "Speaking to yourselves in psalms and hymns and spiritual songs, singing and making melody in your heart to the Lord; [20] Giving thanks always for all things unto God and the Father in the name of our Lord Jesus Christ." Come on, and let us go in!

A prayer of repentance and confession.

Father, I pray that you will forgive me for not making you first. I ask you to forgive me for not making time hear your voice. I know I have been doing a lot of things wrong things, going to wrong places, and saying wrong things. Now I'm ready to be still and know that you are God. I thank you for not giving up on me. I thank you for giving me a hunger and thirst for you. I will no longer waste time waiting until I get in a church setting. I will know you in the power of your might. I thank you for renewing my mind and redeeming the time. Father you are my strength and my salvation. You are my help in the time trouble. I will be balanced and I will pant after you like a dear panted after the water brook. In the name of Jesus!

Life Changing Application

I have provided basic steps to enhance our relationship with God.
1. Commit to prayer 15 minutes a day.
2. Study one scripture at a time.
3. Select a special place to listen to God.
4. Revisit Scriptures from this chapter Isaiah 59:1-2; Exodus 30:10; Hebrews 9:7; and Leviticus Chapter 16.
5. Remain thankful and with a heart of repentance.
6. Live with expectations so faith can be active.
7. Seek God through prayer and memorized scriptures.
8. Avoid the approval of man.
9. Study Jeremiah 29:13; 2 Chronicles 7:14; and Revelations 3:20 for devotional scripture.

Chapter 2

POWER AND AUTHORITY IN GOD'S PRESENCE

*I*n today's society several people lean toward celebrities as role models. Well-known sport players, singers, and actors are idolized as being powerful and enormously wealthy. Various crowds are willing to pay large sums of money just to be in their presence. They depart with no life improvements or added qualities. Power can be defined in a variety of ways: leadership, physical strength, intellectualism, or a supply of energy. Every person has become reliant on some sort of electronic device. They all depend on a source of power to function. Gadgets are constantly being up-graded with the intent of fulfilling the voids of people. There are no comparisons to the power and authority gained while in the presence of God. Time spent with God is an investment that brings immeasurable profits. Your communion with him is more than a gamble, hoping you have a winning ticket. It is definitely a sure guarantee of personal access, heavenly treasures, and God's abundant possession on earth. (Ps. 24:1-2) We can enter into God's presence and have a personal conversation with the King of kings. He never sleeps, and He never slumbers. Neither is his ear too heavy that he cannot hear. Every hour can be spent in the presence of the King of kings. Just the sound of a whisper can get his attention.

How expensive is our spiritual phone bill? Do we talk to God everyday or only when there are 911 urgent needs? If someone else had to survive from your prayers how long would they live? Put your heavenly access into action by using God's word in prayer for yourself and others. 1 Corinthian 9 states: "But I keep under my body, and bring it into subjection: lest that by any means, when I have preached to others, I myself should be a castaway." Matthew 6:10 reminds us that God created everything under the heaven and beneath the earth by his spoken words. His words agreed with his visions and they became creative. When we are in alignment with God, we become the mouthpiece and the pen of a ready writer. God spoke light and it became light. He first said it, and now we see it. What are we speaking? What are our visions? Do your words agree with the vision? God has given us the same creative ability through the bible. Romans 4:17 tells us to speak your vision into reality even though you don't see it, can't touch, can't smell it, or hear sounds of evidence. Keep trusting and believing. God has given us the authority, dominion, and power to speak his word into any situation. In the name of Jesus we can command things to come in agreement with what God's word says.

There is power and authority in the presence of God. Faith will thrust our desire into manifestation. Vision has no concept of time, defeat, or impossibilities. Faith will guide visions toward attainment. Those who trust in Christ walk by faith and not by sight. We focus our attention on the end result not the current conditions. We realize the process is preparing us for the promise. Observing things from the natural sight will cause one to fall into the trap of carnality, instability, and confusion. Faith will keep us focused, steadfast and orderly. Faith believers get ready to reap the harvest and celebrate the fruit of their labor. The natural sight demands explanations, expects speedy results, maintains calculations, and compares deficiencies. Faith has pre-adventure ability to produce the will of God. The natural eye was not created to see the supernatural but witness the manifestation. The testimony of others gives us a sneak preview of what God can do. Witnesses ensure that all the peaks and valleys work together for our good. Faith gives us enough hope to overrule the evidence. Faith exceeds, excels, and propels God's divine power beyond our natural capacity. If God said it, I believe it and there is nothing anyone can do to paralyze or revoke his will.

I often think about the invisible force of God's power to move, reposition, re-establish reform, reorganize and rearrange hopelessness. The Hebrew word for faith is *aman* that means to relinquish all your ability and depend on God. Amen is derived from the word *aman*. God has unlimited power, wisdom, and promises. Our natural abilities are limited. Generally after every prayer is said, every scripture read or testimony shared, the word *amen* seals the deal. When we used the word amen it simply means we agree, rely, and trust that our faith in God is not in vain. However faith and obedience are hand and glove that estimate when our hope will manifest. Hebrews 11:1 adds: "Now faith is the substance of things hoped for, the evidence of things not seen."

I can imagine faith being in millions of metal particles and floating in the wind. God has the magnetic power to pull them together and form objects, places, people and things. How do I get this kind of faith? Romans 4:17 tells us: "So then faith cometh by hearing, and hearing by the word of God." There are benefits of regular fellowship in worship services. However a personal relationship with God begins individually.

Ladies and gentlemen, faith is the currency that purchases all our needs, dreams, and miracles. God has given every man a measure of faith but the growth of it depends on the risk we are willing to make or take with it. Faith in the word is always sufficient for our needs, but it must be activated. God is searching the earth to identify with what is in his image that is connecting with his words so he can manifest his power. Just as a baby must be joined to the umbilical cord, we must be connected to the true vine. He desires to put his creation back into its original state before sin entered into the earth.

It's time to send heavenly signals and release the aroma from his word through prayer so the window of heaven can open. Conquerors are soldiers that pray for the kingdom to come to earth as it is in heaven. The more we talk to God, the more God will respond with evidence. God's delight is in the prayer of the righteous, and Psalms 16:11 (KVJ) goes on to state: "Thou wilt shew me the path of life; in thy presence is fullness of joy; at thy right hand there are pleasures for evermore."

What does this scripture mean, "To be in the presence of God there is fullness of joy"? While in the presence of God nothing else matters. Being in the presence of God fills all the voids and recharges our zeal. His presence calms all fears and permits us to appear before him imperfect and releases us perfected. The presence of God is as simple as the presence of a hospital, a gas station, or even an elementary school.

Faith stimulates God's presences and reflects the attributes of the Holy Spirit. Each of us has been given the power to plant seeds of faith; another person can water it, but we wait on God for the increase. We must not allow the mustard seed to remain small. God is seeking those who will echo his voice and worship him in spirit and in truth. Seek God with high pursuit, reverence, honor, respect, and appreciation. God uses those that will follow his instructions and use His tools and His methods. It may seem a little strange that I would put so much emphasis on faith and prayer. However it is impossible to operate in the realm of God's power and authority without them.

Unfortunately, that comes with long suffering, perseverance, and self-denial. In spite of the offensive components, God's power is able to sustain and gain the victory every time! God desires to see his glory released in the earth. God is the same yesterday, today, and forever. His spirit is living, moving and available. Ephesians 2:10 tells us: "For we are his workmanship, created in Christ Jesus for good works, which God prepared beforehand, that we should walk in them."

Behold God has given Luke 10:19 (KVJ) follows with: "Behold, I give you the authority to trample on serpents and scorpions, and over all the power of the enemy, and nothing shall by any means hurt you. Finally, Matthew 16:19 culminates with: "And I will give unto thee the keys of the kingdom of heaven: and whatsoever thou shalt bind on earth shall be bound in heaven: and whatsoever thou shalt loose on earth shall be loosed in heaven. This is the delegated power and authority we possess being in the presence of God."

The presence of God is available to all who will worship him in spirit and in truth. Operating and functioning in gifts, fruit, and ministries of God must be approved by the use of His power and authority. Many times we become complacent, we are not mindful that it is a privilege and honor to enter into the presence of God. No longer are we required to come before him with turtledoves, virgin goats, or any other animal sacrificial offering for our sin.

We must become more educated in the things of God and be confident sharing the good news with people everywhere. 2 Timothy 2:15 (KVJ) tells us to study to show ourselves approved workman that needeth not to be ashamed, rightly dividing the word of truth.

I pondered the letters of the word *study* and believe the Holy Spirit revealed this acrostic: S.T.U.D.Y., which stands for Strategic Tactics Undoing & Destroying Yokes. Hosea 4:6 adds: "My people are destroyed for lack of knowledge: because thou hast rejected knowledge, I will also reject thee, that thou shalt be no priest to me: seeing thou hast forgotten the law of thy God, I will also forget thy children."

I just recently started my Master's Degree and the first class was geared toward learning styles. God is so amazing. He will go to extreme measures to equip us for His journey. I discovered that the same learning styles can related to the way we study the word of God.

It has been discovered that people learn three different ways: audio, visual, and kinesthetic. What exactly does that mean? The audio learners need to hear a scripture or sermon several times to grasp the message. Information that is recited, pondered, written, or typed is characteristics of an audio learner. The word of God is the core of every aspect of being a Christian. Self-application in the word of God determines the level of heavenly access, spiritual growth, and demonstration of the fruit of the spirit. The audio learner can hear God's voice and respond with confidence.

Visual learners maintain knowledge by images. They may need to view credible Christian videos, illustrations, or demonstrations to understand the word of God. Visual learners can be considered those who witness the process of an individual's testimony and be encouraged to sustain. We are now in the twenty-first century and the word of God is shared in many different features. The word of God catapults every victory and demolition weapon of the enemy. Learning God's word allows people to have an advantage and resistance to temptation. The shield of faith has the ability to quench fiery darts and overthrow pessimism. (Eph. 6:16 KVJ)

The kinesthetic learners extract information by experience or being actively involved. I really like the story in John 20:24-29: Now Thomas (also known as Didymus[)], one of the Twelve, was not with the disciples when Jesus came. So the other disciples told him, "We have seen the Lord!" But he said to them, "Unless I see the nail marks in his hands and put my finger where the nails were, and put my hand into his side, I will not believe." A week later his disciples were in the house again, and Thomas was with them. Though the doors were locked, Jesus came and stood among them and said, "Peace be with you!" Then he said to Thomas, "Put your finger here; see my hands. Reach out your hand and put it into my side. Stop doubting and believe."

Thomas said to him, "My Lord and my God!" Then Jesus told him, "Because you have seen me, you have believed; blessed are those who have not seen and yet have believed."

I don't necessarily see Thomas being a doubter, but maybe he was a kinesthetic learner. Physical contact, or being actively involved, can awaken some people. Once the word of God has taken root it causes spiritual change from the inside out. Constant faith will not prevail against gloomy days because of divorce, nervous breakdowns, co-dependency, behavior disorders, or any other avenues of distress. I refuse to repeat my childhood experience.

I refuse live a life of resentment. I refuse to be captivated by the trauma I encountered. Maybe you are facing some life challenges such as cancer, bankruptcy, identity crisis, low self-esteem, or perhaps you have everything and still feel empty. For this, I refer to this verse: 1 Corinthians 2:9 "Eyes have not seen, nor ear heard, neither have enter into the heart of man the things which God hath prepared for them that love him."

I believe in God for a better life and the best is yet to come. I never thought I would have the opportunity to live in foreign countries, but here I am in Seoul, Korea. I'm the Co-Pastor of people from Africa, Philippines, Germany, and the United States.

The enemy knows that if we can get pass the brokenness, God will mend us toward greatness. In life we will face peaks and valleys but God is always in the mold to rescue, restore, and revive us. Seek the Lord for guidance. Ask Him for direction to the right church so growth can take its course. Sometimes medical attention is necessary, don't just sit and do nothing. Get recharged and release your potential in God's presence. Seek power to get out of debt, power to put the past behind, power to dream big, or power to do something for God that has never been done before. Attain power that will pave the way for others, leave a positive legacy, prepare a spiritual inheritance, and build trust in God like never before. Take authority over every weakness, stronghold, or inability by using the Biblical applications. The power I'm referring to is the boldness to legally use Jesus's name. Enthusiasm to pray with expectation will cause a spiritual explosion.

Place of Communion/Prayer: I am a walking, speaking, and living ark of the covenant. The spirit of God resides in me. I am what God says I am. I can do what he says I can. I can do all things through Christ and that strengthens me. He is greater in me than anything the enemy can bring against me. Lord, I thank you for mountain moving faith. I thank you for power and authority through you and for your purpose. I repent and turn from all my habits and temporary satisfactions. I will be honest with myself and become transparent with you. I will not allow my own inadequacies, defeat, derailments, or disobedience to hinder me from my destiny. I realize that I am God's dwelling place. I have supernatural eyesight to strive for the conclusion of the whole matter. In the name of Jesus, Amen.

Life Changing Applications

It doesn't matter how much we are blessed spiritually or materialistically. We must not forget where God has brought us. I have listed relative objectives that will remind us that we need God and must be one with him.

1. Walk in the spirit of humility.
2. Implement the learning style that best fit your mold.
3. Use creative words that build.
4. Ensure that your eyes, ears, mouth are on one accord.

Chapter 3

THE MINDSET
OF A CONQUEROR

he thoughts of a conqueror should always set on the victory. I was ashamed of my living environment during my childhood. On the other hand, grateful I had a place to call home. I mentioned earlier that things were challenging for me. However, I always had my mind geared toward a new image for my family. In other words, I was being the curse breaker for my family. I saw myself as the first homeowner, business owner, college graduate, author, Psalmist, and soldier in the army of the Lord. Although there have been many struggles and distractions, I believed that God was going to turn things around in my favor. God did that and much more. Being in a place of pain and suffering is a very uncomfortable position. However, it is in that place God can perform miracles, reveal his presence, and demonstrate his power. We serve an amazing God that made it possible for every believer to overcome. He knows how to relieve the agony of pain. He is the master healer, miracle specialist, and the rescuer for all those in captivity.

Conquerors never focus on defeat, disadvantages, inadequacies, or opposition. We target our strategies on completing the process. Someone may be reading this book and may have lost a job, home, car, child, hair, teeth, marriage, diamond ring, keys, or perhaps money, but thanks be to God, you didn't lose your mind.

Praise the name of the Lord! Grace transforms and reestablishes God's original plan in our lives. Notice that there are many storms but the sky remains and wind continues to flow. It assures us that success is available as long as we are alive.

Transformed minds think on things that are pure, holy, and of a good report. Conquerors overthrow negativity and see the positive in spite of the situation. Our thought process must soar above our problems. The process may not allow us to be happy and smile along the way but it shouldn't change our stance. It always seems easier encouraging others until the hardship is experienced personally. The human phase will take its course, through crying and snorting, but along the way we bounce back into our expected results.

Every seed produces after its own kind. Every word we speak is a seed, which falls in the category of positive or negative. Positive words are life and can be seen as building blocks that create a masterpiece. Negative words will cause death, remove hopes, and strip morale. We must realize that the words we speak today are the life we live tomorrow. That's the reason why declarations, decrees, proclamations, and supplications should be spoken daily. We have the power to predict our future by the things we mediate on in conjunction with our conversations. The mind of the conqueror is always willing to admit errors and immediately apply corrective measures. True winners know who they are in God without the praise or acceptance of men. We have no problem dimming the light on ourselves to make others shine brighter. The mindset of a conqueror understands what it means to be crushed, to get the wine, pressed to receive fresh oil, and the birthing process to receive the wheat, according to Joel 24. I have been married for 26 years and discovered that it is much easier to speak positive about my husband Vernon when things are peaches and cream. The words I speak about him in the bad times dictate our future relationship. The commitment we make to God should not only be based on blessings, promises, and inheritances during our mountain experience. We should remain faithful during wilderness and desert experiences. Applying the word of God and confessing the word of God along with treating others the way we should are the attributes of a conqueror.

The word of God can bombard heaven and shake the earth. The word of God is an automatic missile that destroys the enemy and his weapons. The mindset of a conqueror is to walk upright. They foresee themselves somewhere in the future and things are much better than it looks right now. Everybody goes through things in life that are unexpected. I believe that my experience as an only child prepared me for my Christian lifestyle. God makes decisions that we are not courageous enough to make on our own. We become too comfortable with the familiar and become mediocre, complacent, and lose focus on God. God loves to give his children spiritual promotions but they come after the process. Every opposition is a realm of opportunity to gain ground for the kingdom of God.

God knew that when David conquered the lion and the bear, he could defeat Goliath. David never saw himself unworthy or unqualified. He was fully convinced that the name of the Lord Jesus Christ could fill in all his gaps. David did not focus on his natural ability but God's supernatural power. He didn't look at his age, size, or being overlooked. He saw himself soar like an eagle. David's faith connected to the promise that was spoken over him from the foundation of the world. God said in Genesis 1:26 (KJV): "I give you power, dominion, authority over fish of the sea, beast of the field and over everything that creepth upon the earth." The sword, spear, or the javelin that was in Goliath's hand didn't move David.

Today you may be facing a Goliath such as smoking, alcoholism, abuse, low self-esteem, or insecurities. We must see ourselves just as David, although he defeated many giants he still struggled within some areas. God want us to be victorious over every battle. Being an overcomer generates a profile for those struggling in the same areas to know that a day of triumph is at hand. A person trying to get in shape contends with pain and discomfort to accomplish their goals. God does not desire for us to remain in victories from the past but to also prepare us for those in the future. Counting it all joy allows us the power to endure hardship as a good soldier. Remember that liquids are filled up in containers from the bottom to the top. God will pour freshness in our souls to move us forward and closer to his plans for our lives.

Recently, I saw image of the process to make wine. There were images of people stepping on grapes with their bare feet. How gross does that sound? But the final result produced a valuable source. Fruit can always look good when they are detected a far off but the flavor and the sweet aroma makes the difference. When the odds are against us and it appears to be no way out, that's when conquerors are geared up for the challenge. The outer layer and some would even say the outer courts takes place when sin is exposed. The brazen alter and brazen laver is the main parts of the outer courts. The brazen alter is the place of sacrifice. Jesus crucifixion was the sacrifice for the sins of the world. He was perfect and knew no sin. He knew the conclusion of the whole matter. His submission to the father demonstrated the results of endurance.

The brazen laver was necessary for purification. The priest had washed their hands in the brazen laver to show that they were in the position to intercede. Each application was for the sake of others. Whenever the plan of God is deviated by blurred vision or warped thinking, self-destruction is experienced.

We must allow our selfish ambitions to be crushed like fresh grapes. We will need the fruit of the spirit along with the whole armor of God. The fruits of the spirit are love, joy, peace, forbearance, kindness, goodness, faithfulness, gentleness, and self-control. (Gal. 5:22 KJV) In most cases, we allow the spirit of offense and un-forgiveness as a veil or blinder to avoid seeing ourselves. God wants every part of us from the inside out and from top to bottom.

Ephesians 6:10-18 (KJV) states:

> [10] Finally, be strong in the Lord and in his mighty power. [11] Put on the full armor of God, so that you can take your stand against the devil's schemes. [12] For our struggle is not against flesh and blood, but against the rulers, against the authorities, against the powers of this dark world and against the spiritual forces of evil in the heavenly realms. [13] Therefore put on the full armor of God, so that when the day of evil comes, you may be able to stand your ground, and after you have done everything, to stand. [14] Stand firm then, with the belt of truth buckled around your waist, with the breastplate of righteousness in place, [15] and with your feet fitted with the readiness that comes from the gospel of peace. [16] In addition to all this, take up the shield of faith, with which you can extinguish all the flaming arrows of the evil one. [17] Take the helmet of salvation and the sword of the Spirit, which is the word of God. [18] And pray in the Spirit on all occasions with all kinds of prayers and requests.

It is a personal choice to give up if there is no faith, future goals, or the tenacity.

Jesus Christ was faced with challenges on earth and always responded as a conqueror.

We must see ourselves in the finish line regardless of what part of the process we maybe in. We must be confident that God has entrusted us with a portion of himself in the word of God. We are walking conduits for the Holy Spirit to operate in the earth. We are mechanisms that God expects to be creative, generate productivity, and combat the weapons of the enemy. We are more than conquerors; we are winners at all the times. It is not based on worldly possession or the popularity of men but the position which God has called us in. The process begins with the willingness to open up, empty out, and be totally honest with ourselves.

Realize that we are nothing without God. It is in him that we move, live, and breathe. In other words, we are non-existent. Know that we have promised moments, times of harvest, and dominating victory. There is a process and some of those phases consist of winter seasons, desert walks and even valley experiences. However, the dark moments are necessary. If we could only realize that the righteous must suffer persecution. It doesn't matter whether those hard places are caused by unwise decisions, we can complete the process and come out with a testimony.

When the total of what was self inflicted or trauma from outside interference the end result will always work together for our good. The reflection of how it could have been worse counteracts the fact that we overcame. It groomed us into what we are today. It enhanced our prayers for those that remain in the war zone. It gave us the assurance that God answers prayers. It conditioned for future battles.

It may have not sounded; felt like it and most definitely didn't look like what was desired. Our experiences teach valuable lessons, nourish those in pain, and give factual evidence that Jesus never leaves us even midst of our crisis. The mind of a conqueror gains secure control over their weakness, inadequacies, setbacks, and disadvantages. The mind of Christ is developed by significant events, occurrences, and changes. They are all necessary to have a true effective testimony. God uses basic fundamentals with applications that lead us in the path of success!

A place of Communion: Lord, give me the strength to elevate my mind beyond what I can see or touch. Help me know that I'm your spoken word with a purpose of glorifying you. I confess that I have not been steadfast in my faith. Give the strategy to fulfill my dreams, visions, or goals. Thank you for being patient, forgiving, and granting me time and favor. I understand that obstacles, trials, and tribulations come to prepare me for destiny. There is no weapon formed again me that is able to defeat a conqueror like me. I will see myself as a champion at all time.

Life Changing Application

Often times we don't realize the effect our words and thoughts have on our situations. These are just a few tools that will create a positive outcome.

1. Speak the promises of God over my life and everything I'm affiliated with.
2. Make declarations against the battles I'm facing.
3. Be committed to victory.
4. Repent for any negative words spoken
5. Don't compare the process to present condition.
6. Give God the glory in advance for the finished product.

Chapter 4

THE BENEFITS OF DILIGENCE, DISCIPLINE, AND DETERMINATION

*D*uring my experiences with God I developed three steps that are guiding me to fulfill my dreams. I call them the 3D approach. Diligence is like pounding a nail with a hammer until a house is built. Discipline is the willpower to resist satisfying desires. Determination is self- motivation that opposes the odds.

There are great similarities with the 3D glasses used for movies to my 3D approach. Advantages of the 3D glasses present almost realistic objects that appear touchable with a compelling effect. They present accuracy, brighter lighting, synchronization, and moving objects faster than the natural eye can see. The 3D approach requires intense force to transform dreams into reality. Despite the fact that struggles have taken place, they can be used as part of the process. The 3D approach gives us the ability to take part and just experience special animated affects.

Our goals in life can truly advance if we are driven with the 3D approach. We should include God as we go with our daily routine. Most people have the same daily activities such as: showering, brushing teeth, using deodorant, getting dressed, and making sure our hair is in place. Some people have breakfast, maybe just a cup of coffee, and then off to work, school, gym, or parental activities. God is standing by the way side wondering when will it be his turn? When will He get chance to take part in our schedule? God is faithful under all circumstances.

Diligence is pursuing with vigor until the job is completed with excellence. Jesus Christ is the perfect example of diligence. He understood his assignment from God the father. He remained focused regardless of the rejection, disappointment, manipulation, deception, and not to mention his crucifixion. He never lost his motivation, joy, peace, or tenacity to finish his purpose for mankind and God. Everything Jesus handled in his daily routine was with excellence. Although He may not operate in our timeframe or use methods of our choice, the results of Jesus exceed our expectations. Unlike some of us today, who generally want what's quick and painless. Jesus only did what the father instructed. He made himself submissive to the one who sent him. He prayed to the father that was in heaven. He demonstrated the lifestyle of dominion, power, and authority while living in the flesh. He was careful and humble while confronting the enemy and interacting with people. He showed no partiality between the poor, rich, children, adults or status of dignitaries. Jesus demonstrated diligence in every aspect of his actions.

Being disciplined is not an automatic chain of reaction. It requires self-denial, developed structure, and a reflection of one's integrity. Self-control will restrain the response of temporary satisfaction. There is an area of restraints against distraction through trail, temptation, and the influence of worldly seductions. Discipline is the application of being governed by the Holy Spirit. It takes the Spirit of the living God to live by the commandments, statures, and ordnances of God. If discipline is applied without God, a person is subject to wavering, becoming unstable, double minded, inconsistent, and confused.

I can remember the first time I fasted for three days. I had such a great expectation of being used by God in a supernatural and miraculous manner. I had no idea God was pruning, purging and purifying every part of my being to serve him with my whole heart. There were areas in my life that were hindering me from operating in the full potential intended by God. There is a false hope to expect God to be pleased with our service when we trespass God's plan, when we speak without permission, when we go places with the consent of God.

We must be kingdom minded and not seek the popularity of men. The purpose of discipline will grant a realm of authority with a lifestyle of standards and testimonies. Equal ingredients of discipline, dedication, and determination are absolute prerequisites for a lifestyle of Holiness. All these application rely on personal choices. Joshua 24:15 (KJV) states: "And if it seem evil unto you to serve the Lord, choose you this day whom ye will serve; whether the gods which your fathers served that were on the other side of the flood, or the gods of the Amorites, in whose land ye dwell: but as for me and my house, we will serve the Lord."

I am determined to never repeat my childhood experiences as an adult. I got married at the age of 18 years old, exactly one week after graduation. I always had the desire to be self-employed. I traveled 12 hours to take my state board exam and failed several times before I passed. I knew I had the gift and refused to allow an examination to disqualify me from my goal. I completed my state board exam and became a license cosmetologist in the state of Arkansas. We cannot use our inadequacies to eliminate us from destiny. If I had allowed my unsatisfactory score to keep me from receiving my license, I would never have the privilege of owning three salons at the same time and using those facilities to minister to women. I created a Christian atmosphere, playing praise and worship music. It is a skill I use everywhere I go.

We must use the scars of pain and agony as reminders to show the enemy its plans were unsuccessful. James 2:26 tells us: "For as the body without the spirit is dead, so faith without works is dead." God never intended for us to confine ourselves to limited opportunities. His will is to open windows of heaven unto us.

Everything we do should prosper; we have the option of being entrepreneurs.

I would have never obtained my Master Instructor license. We determined that if the enemy is invested this much time to stop me, there must be a pot of gold at the end of the tunnel. God blessed me with a gift.

My determination launched a new generation for my lineage. Determination is the fuel that will drive you through any storm and won't accept the words "not possible" as the final answer. Statistics predict the future of those that cannot overcome life traumas. A strong will to press past pain and use it as stepping stones will make anyone a better person.

I believe God determines the level of trust, responsibility, and integrity by the level of our determination. The constant and continuous efforts develop faithfulness. Malachi 3:9-11 reads: "Bring ye all the tithes into the storehouse, that there may be meat in mine house, and prove me now herewith, saith the Lord of hosts, if I will not open you the windows of heaven, and pour you out a blessing, that there shall not be room enough to receive it. [11] And I will rebuke the devourer for your sakes, and he shall not destroy the fruits of your ground; neither shall your vine cast her fruit before the time in the field, saith the Lord of hosts." God has promised that our determination in prayer, fasting, living holy, and proclaiming his name are not in vain. Put your faith to work and give it an assignment! Matthew 21:21 says: [21] So Jesus answered and said to them, "Assuredly, I say to you, if you have faith and do not doubt, you will not only do what was done to the fig tree, but also if you say to this mountain, 'Be removed and be cast into the sea,' it will be done."

It was always in desperate situations when Jesus appeared on the scene. For example, Jesus performed the first miracle after they ran out of wine. The Zaraphath woman said, " *As* the LORD thy God liveth, I have not a cake, but an handful of meal in a barrel, and a little oil in a cruse: and, behold, I *am* gathering two sticks, that I may go in and dress it for me and my son, that we may eat it, and die". (John 2:3 NASV) However, after she exhausted down to the bare minimum, God used the prophet for a lifetime supply. Jesus was determined to please the father. After he took thirty-nine lashes, his hands and feet were nailed. He endured the crown of thorns on his head and felt a spear pierce his side. He echoed that his mission was completed, stating: "He said it is finished." Jesus exerted every ounce of energy so we could have him omnipresent.

My grandmother was all in one to me. She was my sister, mother, role model and father. Although she had little to work with, she displayed a diligence to keep me school. I could have easily been discouraged because I had no parental visibility at my school activities. I focused on the fact that she was compelling me to be a High School graduate. She was disciplined enough to keep a job, although there was a struggle with alcohol, limited resources, and little intellect. She taught me how to survive through her brokenness, common sense, and past failures. I felt the love and responsibility and burden of relying on God to help us during the many crises we faced. She was determined to make sure I went to church every Sunday, even though she didn't attend.

She knew God's power could make a difference on me and I could receive something from church that she could never provide. I embraced every cycle of hardship we shared together. I give God the praise and I continuously thank Him for sowing her into my life. The first time my mother and grandmother ever attended any school function was my graduation at El Dorado High School. Wow, it was so exciting and very emotional event for me. While my classmates were joyous and receiving graduation gifts, taking pictures along with all capstones, I couldn't stop thanking God from inside for allowing me to make history right before two witnesses that made it possible in spite of all the oppositions we faced together. I received a portion of God's benefits from being diligent, disciplined, and determined.

God expects us to be dedicated every part of our lives. He searches to find himself in us. We can be faithful to God with our time, treasures, and talents. We all have natural gifts. All natural talents were given to us even in our mother's womb. Every good and perfect gift comes from God. God uses our time, treasures, and talents to draw people, establish wealth, and redeem time. Outsiders will observe and bear witness the presence of God. Opportunity is revealed when we are being diligent, dedicated, and disciplined. We must remember only what we do for Christ will last.

There is an orchestrated sound to be released from your talents, treasures, and time that only you can produce. No one else can duplicate what God has placed within you. God is calling us closer; God desires to have a personal relationship with his children. God is searching the earth for the echoes of his word by the life we live.

Our talents, treasures, and time are very diverse and not limited to a Christian office, functions, or positions. We need the light of Jesus Christ everywhere through doctors, lawyers' governors, teachers, principals, supervisors, police offices, and firemen. The list can goes on and on of the multiple ways we receive services from someone talents. When God blesses us with a passion, there is a mandate for it. What God has for you it is for you but others are blessed in the process.

What if all the doctors decided to go on strike? What if all the police officers decided that they no longer wanted to put their lives in danger? What if the mechanics decided they no longer want to go home smelling like oil and gas? What if your childcare provider decided that they only take care of their own children? What if God decided on the fifth day that he was tired and had already worked four days? What if Jesus after he carried his cross decided that he was not going to let them crucify him? I believe my point is made with how we are accommodated by those who are using their talent, treasures, and time.

Perhaps you are not sure about your purpose in life? Where to find your treasures? How to invest your time? I believe God's voice behind the word of God revealed methods to navigate his people toward destiny. God's will is for us to know his word. When we read what the word of God says we are exposed to the power and authority he has given us, and it will stir up the gifts within. His delight is in our obedience, which in turn gives us the desires of our heart. What is it that you really enjoy doing? Are you very good at it? Have never been taught? Is it cooking, cleaning, speaking, decorating, dancing, or singing? Whatever it is, you can do with a spirit of excellence without a lot of effort. You find pleasure, peace, excitement, and creativity in the process. The talent that you possess is the plan or intent of God for your life. Jeremiah 29:11 says: "God knows the plans he has for you." His plan or intent is your purpose in life that produces passion, passion produces prosperity, and prosperity leads us to the promise. The promises of God unfold prophecies, which lead us toward our inheritance. Now, give God praise if you can!

We must make Jesus first. It's not always necessary to pray on your knees, create a charismatic atmosphere, or quote a lot of scriptures. The moment we open our eyes from night of rest, just tell God thank you! When our feet touch the floor, we should ask God to order our steps for that day. When you get in the shower, ask God to cleanse you from all unrighteousness. While you are brushing your teeth, think of prophetic things you desire to happen for the day. When you are getting dressed, put on the whole amour of God. The moment you leave home, you are fully equipped to do the work of the Lord. You are fully equipped to resist the enemy. At any point of when fleshly activities try to arise, the Holy Spirit is present to convict and is willing to restore.

Try, try, and try again! No big deal if you didn't succeed the first, second, third or fourth time. Maybe you feel abandoned, inferior, financially insufficient, frustrated, and fatigued. Use the resources you haveand network. Don't be afraid to ask for help.

Rekindle your interest. Realize that miracles are still happening, especially to those that don't give up!

God's promises to us support if we push pass our natural ability to experience a mighty move of his power. You can lose weight! You can own your business! You can be a bestselling author! You can get your education! You can learn the word of God! You can preach the Gospel! You can purchase items in full and be debt free! There are so many other accomplishments to be achieved with the application of Diligence, Discipline, and Determination. What are you waiting for? Get started today! There is victory in the end but only if you can weather the storm. The benefits of the three Ds guarantee an arrival at destiny on time. They install a great influence on self-control, faithfulness, and most of all the favor of God! Today is the day that the Lord has made just for us to make it known that there are no limitations if we put our faith in motion. The more evidence we achieve allocates us the ability to share with others.

A Place of Communion

Father, I pray that you will forgive me for my unbelief. I repent for not using my gift. I pray that I can expand my faith toward things beyond my natural ability. Lord, gives me the strength to overcome my obstacles. I thank you for hind's feet to run through troops and leap over walls. I thank you for patience during my process so I can gain wisdom and knowledge to maintain my place of destiny. Forgive me for not realizing the investment you made in me. Forgive me for comparing myself to other people and not accepting that I'm fearfully and wonderfully made, appointed, and approved by you. I will move forward in the things of God with obedience and perseverance.

Life Changing Application

Keeping momentum while being faced with oppositions can be challenging. I have listed seven steps keep your morale high.

1. Write your future plans.
2. Develop short and long term goals.
3. Be persistent with deadlines
4. Don't allow time to be the measure factor.
5. Strive to complete one task at a time.
6. Stay focused by posting pictures of your dreams.
7. Believe that all things are possible, especially for yourself.

Chapter 5

DIVINE TIMING OF GOD

*T*ime is always ticking and nearly everyone has a watch. Every person has places to go and people they desire to see. We all have made specific time s and dates that we look forward to such as birthday, anniversary, graduation, and wedding. God is omnipresent. God is the Alpha and the Omega. One day is a thousand years and a thousand years can be as one day. God is able to redeem, shift, or move time. However, God has a requirement that we must meet out before he can give us spiritual promotions. The divine timing of God is in alignment with a heavenly purpose and plan. He responds by his word but acquainted with our grief. Our emotional state does not get God's attention. God inhabits the praises of his people and seeks those that worship him in spirit and in truth. The time is now for the people of God to get in sync with the rhythm of God. We are currently living in a time when the Christians should join together in unity and operate on one accord.

There is a mandate for revelation, divine information that will remove stagnation and mediocrity. The five fold ministries will be intertwined around the world and function as an army. There is a new generation of warrior and trailblazers in the spirit. They will be unknown, outcast, and those people have given up on. They will hear and obey God, walk upright for God, and will not compromise. This is a season of "Who is that?" It will not be in the form of fame, prestige, or personal financial gain, but to overpower the wiles of the enemy. Although there are wars, catastrophes, terrorist attacks, mass shootings, drive by shootings, along with episodes of things to happen in the last days, God is doing much more, even though it is not broadcast or revealed on a large scale. The enemy can never defeat God's power! We can no longer rely on the ministerial staff to invade Satan's territory. Everyone that proclaims the death, burial, and resurrection of Jesus Christ, should be a threat to the enemy.

We must all reflect the same standard and meet the requirement to be in full operation of what God wants to do in the earth. God does not have a respect person although we are called to specific assignments and purposes. We all apply the same applications to accept Jesus as our personal Savior. We have the same access through prayer to gain power through the word of God according to our faith. We all wrestle not against flesh and blood but principalities in high places. (Eph. 6:12 KJV) We are all targeting the same enemy.

God has given us all the resources, references, and weapons we need to gain victory. Our goal is to arrive in a place called "heaven".

Jesus died for everyone to accept him as our personal Savior. He can reveal his glory through in and throughout our lives. When we make a conscious decision to totally submit to God everyday of our lives, the larger our territory will become in the kingdom of God. During the process of becoming submissive, there will a demand for sacrifices. It is impossible to live Holy without sacrifices things of value. Sacrifices obligate us to deny our will and way to comply with God's level of responsibility. God develops structure that stabilizes our spirit, will, and emotions when we are being consistent toward our commitment. Strategies provide a sense of direction and a better understanding and application of God's word.

While in prayer, God revealed a strategy that will give guidance on the four S's, earlier I mentioned submission, sacrifice, structure and strategy. Fasting is abstinences food, time, electronics, shopping or anything that is rendered as a valuable offering to God. The fasting guide has been a blessing to me, and those who join me.

I first applied the fasting guide in 2006, along with four women from the church where I'm now the Co-Pastor. We all received a closer walk with the Lord, our prayers became more intense, the word began to come alive as we would share what we read among each other. There were many blessings, revelations, and miracles experienced. There were multiple phases of deliverance, purging, and pruning that also took place. I know that you will have the same testimonies. I have always fasted periodically but never as a consistent lifestyle.

Each time I have fasted God has granted me the privilege of spiritual maturity. I had expectations of what God was going to do. In January 2001, I believed that God was challenging me to fast for an extended period of time. I heard God say it's time for a forty day fast. Immediately I thought I was going die of starvation. At that time I had never heard of the Daniel fast, which saved my life and attitude toward my obedience to God's request. I thought I would raise the dead, lay hands on the sick, and they would be instantly healed. I thought I would walk through the hospital and just by the power of God recover all those admitted. I thought this was the time God was going to use me to show the world that he was large and in charge. Needless to say, I do believe that there are times that all my thoughts will come to pass. Unfortunately, that is not what God was preparing me for. Nine days after the fast was completed, my mother died. She passed away from a heart attack on Februarys 17, 2001 — the day after my birthday.

Our relationship was just beginning to soar and so was her relationship with God. There I was left to make all the funeral arrangements along with carrying out my mother's request. I styled my mother's hair and made sure her final exit was with class and elegance. I believe that through the time of fasting, God prepared me to operate from the supernatural realm and do what was required for me as "the only child". I recognized that living a life of consecration includes the natural and spiritual channels for us to operate. Just because we offer God sacrifices does not give us the right to manipulate God. It does not give us control over God with instruction of when, where, how, or explanations of why he should carry out our plans.

God is not impressed with temporary vows we make as if he is an auction appealer. He is mesmerized by the sincerity of our hearts to please him. Sacrificial offering prepares us to maneuver and display a Christ-like attitude under pressure. I'm not portraying that I was superwomen or was desensitized to the loss of my mother but I know that it was the sacrifice I rendered to God that allowed me to go through it. I know the benefits of rendering sacrificial offerings to God permit the fruit of the spirit to get nourishment and our spiritual gifts can be cultivated. Fasting dismantle those things that hinder us from spiritual growth and permits us to be receptive to correction.

Remember that without correction there can be no perfection. Rebuke does not feel good to your emotions but it healing to the soul. We must never perceive correction to be offensive even if it's not done in the right tone. I had surgery June 3rd, 2013, and immediately connected to this chapter. The first step was called the preoperative fasting that required me to go without eating or drinking for a twenty-four hour period. The purpose for the absence of food and fluid were to eliminate me from pulmonary aspiration. Next was intra-operative care that transfers me to the operating room, which is referred to as (PACU) Post-Operative Anesthesia Care Unit. They inserted several IVs to prepare me for surgery with anesthesia and be prepped and draped for surgery. The nurse secured safety precautions against possible infection prevention and possible physiological reactions. The final phase of the surgery was to remain in the recovery room before I could be released to my room or home. If we want to be made whole in Christ Jesus there must be a period of spiritual renovation, upgrade, and modification.

My experience of heart surgery displayed that all Christians must be willing to comply with God's red-print; Jesus's spoken word, to gain spiritual growth and access to the heavenly realm. The phases of the surgery preparation have many similarities with what takes place during the sacrificial offering to God. It took me to deny the temptation of food and water for the expected results. I had to follow the recommendations from the doctor and confidence in what he said. A transformation should take place not just from location to another room but transform our level of maturity, character, and integrity. After I was released from the hospital I had scarred tissue but within a period of time the scars faded away. In order for me to maintain my wellness I had to change my eating habits, exercise, and become more educated to prevent future altercations. I also had periodic follow-up for observations.

It doesn't matter how good the food or word of God may be—no one wants to be served with soiled utensils. God desires us to be a clean and pure vessel so we don't contaminate the word of God with the works of the flesh. KVJ Matthew 7:21-23 states: Not everyone that saith unto me, Lord, Lord, shall enter into the kingdom of heaven; but he that doeth the will of my Father which is in heaven. Many will say to me in that day, Lord, Lord, have we not prophesied in thy name? And in thy name have cast out devils? And in thy name done many wonderful works? And then will I profess unto them, I never knew you: depart from me, ye that work iniquity. Let us not have the form of Godliness and not possess the true power of living the life completely according to 2 Timothy 3-5 (KJV)

I encourage everyone to render a sacrificial offering to God everyday and it will become a lifestyle. We must always be in position for God to use us at anytime and in any place.

Don't be getting ready but be ready? John F. Kennedy, the 35th President of the United States, once said, "my fellow American, ask not what your country can do for you, ask what you can do for your country" I endeavor to say, "My dear sisters and brothers in Christ, don't expect God to do everything for you, but ask God what would you like me to do for the sake of the kingdom?"

Preparation for Fasting

It is mentioned in Matthew 6:17-18, that we should not allow our countenance to display that we are fasting. Fasting should never be viewed as a diet but every aspect of Christian growth. In this time it can be challenging to proclaim a sabbatical but it can be done with the right plan. A sabbatical according to the scripture was done every seventh year. It was a specific time for one year to focus on a deeper relationship with God and a personal renewal twenty-four hours for 365 days of seeking God. The fasting guide will grant a portion of leading toward a lifestyle of Holiness. Our time of fasting should be centered on prayer targets, scripture base, and start and ending times. Often God will extend the time scheduled.

Fasting should be planned so you have ample time to prepare, organize your schedule, purchase food items, and set your environment for the aim. The fast should be included in your prayers prior and throughout the fast. There are three prayers that will be shared during this chapter: moderate, intercessory, and warfare prayers. The moderate prayer is simple conversation between you and God for food and public places of discrepancies. For example while praying for your food, invocation in areas religious diversity. Praying on the behalf of others is intercessory prayer and is generally done in an arranged area of prayer. For example, most churches have a time of intercessory prayer as part of their order of service. The battleground is speaking the word of God against the enemy.

Pleading the blood of Jesus against everything that is not of God is an example of a warfare prayer. This is the ability to counteract any signs from the enemy that is contrary to the word of God. Pleading the blood of Jesus is simply realizing that the blood that Jesus shed on the cross is still alive and pliable today. The Blood of Jesus is so powerful that it caused a great earthquake, the curtains ripped from top to bottom, and the rocks were split. The blood of Jesus is an undeniable weapon to the enemy.

Prayer is essential for every believer to sustain and maintain the level of God's standards. God's divine timing is directed toward our level of maturity, his assignment and purpose for our lives. Whenever we make wise decisions in the areas of ethos and pathos, we fall in the category of a Karios moment. During our journey of change, seasons, and transitioning, God is teaching us to be as the children of Issachar, the discerners of time. (Gen. 30:14-18 KJV) While going through my childhood ordeals, I always believed that things would get better but I never imagine living in the dream state of Hawaii, Germany, or Korea. Korea is a place where time is always ahead of central time. God is so amazing to distribute the time around the world so people can praise and worship him 24/7 and 365 days a year.

My desire is to walk and live in total obedience to God. In 2005, I had to make a decision of closing a successful seven year established business, departing from my grandmother who was very dear to my heart, telling all my clients that I would no longer be able to be their stylist, and moving miles away from family and friends. Oh, I felt as if God was stripping me of everything I had worked so hard to rebuild. My dream car was practically given away. I gave up the comfort all material things that seemed to restore all my heartbreaks and headaches along with a salary that was simply unbelievable for a country girl from Arkansas that came from nothing. I packed up to support my husband who was being stationed in Seoul, Korea, only to find out on my arrival and getting settled that I could not open a salon.

Lord help me, I instantly slipped in moments of resentment. I started praying and fasting and God revealed this scripture to me: "And Jesus answered and said, 'Assuredly, I say to you, there is no one who has left house or brothers or sisters or father or mother or wife or children or lands, for My sake and the gospel's, who shall not receive a hundredfold now in this time—houses and brothers and sisters and mothers and children and lands, with persecutions—and in the age to come, eternal life." (Mark 10:29-30) I read this scripture every day, several times a day. I began to get an understanding the time and season had shifted. Through much prayer and fasting, God slowly built my clientele again, and they began to sow into me like never before.

Those seeds consisted of large monetary gifts, flat screen televisions, very nice cars, free trips, expensive clothes, and jewelry. The gifts came from complete strangers and some later became members of our local church. God did it again! This time I didn't work as hard as before neither was it something that I prayed for. Our obedience and sacrifice for God to do a spiritual sanitation inspection will prepare us for exceptional accreditations. God began to expand my horizon by placing me around people that were college students. They encouraged me to go back to school. I took their advice and obtained an Associates and a Bachelor degree, along with Certifications of Human Development and Clinical Mental Health. I'm continuing my education to be in a position to minister and educate others. There are so many reasons that are not listed. Why not fast and obtain your own personal testimony? Start today!

There are various benefits of fasting, but the ultimate goal is about individual cleanliness first. It is very important to study the word of God more intensely during this time. Please feel free to study other advantages of fasting.

Demons flee (Matt. 17:21)
National Disaster Adverted (Jon. 3:10)
Visions come (Dan.10:5-6)
Physical Health Restored (Isa. 58:6-8)
Deliverance (Ps. 35:11-14)
Change the Laws (Esther 4:16)

Loose the Bands of wickedness (Isa. 58:6)
Undo heavy Burden (Isa. 58:6)
To let the oppressed go free (Isa. 58:6)
Protection (Isa. 9)

Lifestyle of fasting
Isaiah Chapter 58

January

(All Countries) Corruption and the God fearing people in position. 4 a.m. to 12 Noon (Avoid all fried foods).

February

(Leaders) President, Pastors, Husbands, 5-Fold ministry, all Business owners, Managers, Supervisor, Teachers, Judges, Governors, Mayors, etc. (Daniel Fast)

March

(Evangelism) TV Ministries, Christian books, Gospel CDS, DVDS, Magazines Foreign missionaries, cartoons, movie etc. (No caffeine beverages such as tea, coffee, soda. (The entire month)

April

(Resurrection) Hope, Dreams, Vision, Spiritual gifts, Revelation, Great exploits discovered, etc. (No shopping/necessities only)

May

(Women) Low self esteem pregnancy naturally and spiritually, those in prison, singles, single parents, God fearing mothers and wives. 5AM to 5pm (One meal of your choice along with healthy snacks.

June

(Men) God fearing men of valor, faithfulness, spiritual identity, servant's heart, able to speak the word of God with boldness and purity, humble hearts that please God. Avoid deserts, bread & starchy goods. (Entire month)

July

(Children) Pray against peer pressure, negative influence, abstinences from sexual activity, addictive substance, leadership, Remember children that are in confinement, anger management. Rebellion, respect, honor, teachable spirit. Heart to serve God. Avoid negative words and unnecessary chatting to hear the voice of God. (The entire month)

August

(Pray for those affected by war and all catastrophes) Relationships enrichment, Rehabilitations, Spiritual growth, unhealthy soul ties, Spiritual direction.

5 a.m. to noon (Fruit & Healthy stacks. (Entire month).

September

(Revival) Supernatural outpour, wisdom, knowledge, understanding, obedience to the voice of God. (4 a.m. to 4 p.m.) No theater, TV, Computer or electric device unless it is job related or emergency.

October

(Pray for nonbelievers) All those that worship idols, backsliders, hypocrites, deception, witchcraft, and manipulation. Pray for deliverance, spiritual breakthrough, against strongholds and generation curses. 12 a.m. to noon (Increase your devotional time 30 additional minutes the entire month.

November

(Gratitude) Adoration unto god for who he is and what he means to you. Thank God for all he has already done and going to do. Look around and thank God for nature and the things he has created just supply and soothe our desires. Thank him for the opportunity to worship the only true and living God. (Read Psalms 91 everyday several times a day for the entire month.)

December

(Celebrate) The birth of Jesus Christ, the right to praise and worship his Holy name. Praise God for bringing you to this point in your life. Praise God for being alive, Praise God for your future. Praise God for your generational blessing, Praise God for not leaving us alone. Praise God for everything.

5 a.m. to noon (Please use your own discretion of sacrifice unto the God our salvation).

Please be advised that the fast was given to me by God. I believe it will be a blessing of guidance and discipline for those of interest. However I do understand that it may be adjusted for those on medication. God bless you, and expect to give testimony of what will take place during sacrifices.

I encourage the people of God to study the Jewish calendar and special dates. They have great significance to prophetic movement. We should take the initiative to get the best education we can possibly gain. It will prepare us to have more excellent results. "And the children of Issachar, who were men who had understanding of the times, to know what Israel ought to do." (1 Chron. 12:32 KJV)

The word understanding is the Hebrew word *binah*, which means "to have insight or to act with prudence." According to Strong's Concordance, it comes from a root verb that means to separate something mentally, and distinguish its parts. The word reflects the presence of intelligence and wisdom, even cunning and skill, in the process. In other words, this is not just an under-standing of the facts, but a skillful analysis of what something truly means, how to respond, and when to pursue.

When comes to death, know that those who are already left this earth can possibly be on the other side with Christ, where they will live again. "But I would not have you to be ignorant, brethren, concerning them which are asleep, that ye sorrow not, even as others which have no hope." (1 Thess. 4:13 KJV) We must not assume we are above the laws of this land or become self-exalted as if we are self-sufficient. For I would not, brethren, that ye should be ignorant of this mystery, lest ye should be wise in your own conceits; that blindness in part is happened to Israel, until the fullness of the Gentiles be come in. Consider the ants that are not strong as we are but yet they observe the time and prepare for the winter season. Go to the ant, O sluggard; consider her ways, and be wise. Without having any chief, officer, or ruler, she prepares her bread in summer and gathers her food in harvest. (Prov. 6:6-8) People of the most God, how much more equipped are we, to have an understanding of the "Times".

THERE SO MANY OTHER REASONS NOT LISTED THAT WE SHOULD PRESENT A SACRIFICAL OFFERING, WHY NOT FAST?

The purpose of the monthly fast is to combat the trend of demonic attack.

Most opponents become familiar with their competitor so we as Christians should do the same. Never be deceived. God's will always win regardless of what the world may present. (2 Cor. 2:11) [11] Lest Satan should get an advantage of us: for we are not ignorant of his devices. We should not allow the enemy to have the upper hand or be caught unprepared.

A spiritual war began in heaven between God and Lucifer. In that battle only one king could reign. During the course of action there were a host of angels to witness the controversial action between the two. In my imaginary mind, I believe the battle was not physical but verbally. I believe God predicted his final destination. Lucifer began to brag about all the things he would do and expose ways he deserved to be in charge. Somehow he was able to convince a third of angels in heaven to agree with him and they become a part of his destructive plan.

God is all powerful and is self sufficient. On the other hand Satan is not, he needs the assistance of others. They are divided into categories such as; demons, principalities, princess and familiar spirits. Often times Lucifer is address by many different names these are the most common Satan, Dragon, and Devil. There many others listed in the Bible.

According to Frances Maria Guazzo & Michael Psullus found that Satan army was strategically organized. They consider them as classification by domain. These two authors came to the conclusion that each demonic force has a specific assignment. Their research recapped events from the 1st to the 3rd century known as the testament of Solomon.

Psellus continued to confirm his studies toward the 11th century with witnesses of people who avoided the daylight and saw invisible images. Year later as the curiosity of the classification of demons grew more people became interested.

Alfons De Spina in 1467 added his theory about the classification of demons. During his study, he labeled Satan demonic forces as;

- Demons of fate
- Goblins
- Incubi and succubi
- Wandering groups or armies of demons
- Familiar Spirits
- Drudes

- Demons that are born from the union of a demon with a human being.
- Liar and mischievous demons
- Demons that attack the saints
- Demons that try to induce old women to attend Sabbaths

He enlarged his studies in many different countries which expose insight about legends and stories. He linked the drudes to the German folklore. He said that familiar, goblins and other mischievous demons belong to the folklore of most European countries. The explanation is believed to not be limited spirits can appear where ever there is entrance.

Peter Binsfeld continued to explore about demon classification continued to grow in 1589. He derived his information from the seven deadly sins. Each sin mentioned is luring tactics of temptations.

- Lucifer: pride
- Mammon: greed
- Asmosdeus: lust
- Leviathan: envy
- Beelzebub: gluttony
- Satan/ Amon: wrath
- Belphegor: sloth

Guazzo, Francesco Maria started to compile information from Michael Psellus that was published in his book *Compendium Maleicarum* in 1608. His research make known demonic activity with nature and destruction.

- Demons of the superior layers of the air, which never establish a relationship with people.
- Demons of the inferior layers of the air, which are responsible for storms.

- Demons of earth, which dwell in fields, caves and forests.
- Demons of water, which are female demons, and destroy aquatic animals.
- Demons of the underground part of the earth, responsible of keeping hidden treasures, causing earthquakes, and causing the crumbling of houses.
- Demons of the night, which are black and evil. These demons avoid daylight.

Five years later, Sebastien Michaelis wrote a book, *Admirable History* that shared information about demon classification based on hierarchies. They are known to be sins that influence temptation. He also connects demons names to French and are nameless in other catalogs. The First Hierarchy includes;

- Beelzebub: arrogance; adversary, St. Francis
- Leviathan: attacks Christian religious beliefs; adversary, St. Peter
- Asmodai: lust; adversary: St. John
- Berith: murdering and blasphemy; adversary, St. Barnabas
- Astaroth: laziness and vanity; adversary, St. Bartholomew
- Verrin: impatience; adversary, St. Dominic.
- Gressil: impurity, uncleanness and nastiness; adversary, St. Bernard
- Sonnellon: hate; adversary, St. Stephen.
- Second Hierarchy
- Lilith: first wife of Adam, succubus
- Azazel: the Angel of Death

Third Hierarchy
- Belial: arrogance; adversary, St. Francis of Paula
- Olivier: fierceness, greediness and envy; adversary, St. Lawrence
- Jouvart: sexuality; adversary, not cited.

I believe that each author is revealing the purpose for prayer and fasting. In 1801 Francis barret wrote called the "The Magus." He mentions the classifications of demons and evil attitudes of people and things.   .

- Mammon: seducers
- Asmodai: vile revenges
- Satan: witches and warlocks
- Pithius: liars and liar spirits
- Belieal: fraud and injustice
- Merihem: pestilences and spirits that cause pestilences
- Abaddon: war, evil against good
- Astaroth: inquisitors and accusers

The classification of demonic powers for each month does not list an author. During the 16th century it is believed that each demon gain more strength to accomplish it mission each month. In today terminology it is referred to as horoscope or astrological implications more than religion.

- Belial in January
- Leviathan in February
- Satan in March
- Belphegor in April
- Lucifer in May
- Bertith in June
- Beelzebub in July
- Astaroth in August
- Thammuz in September
- Baal in October
- Asmodia in November
- Moloch in December

My goal is not to promote nor esteem the action of Satan and his follower. The purpose of sharing this information is to prepare the people of God for spiritual warfare. We are soldiers in *the* army of the Lord. We must be aware of the plots, plans and schemes of the enemy. I compelled by the Holy Spirit to share this information. The world is established by many categories of authority. It doesn't matter if it is political, federal judicial, or parental there are a chain of commands. We must strive in constant perfection or our competitors will gain the upper hand. We will become a slave to sin and control by a superficial Master.

> Ephesians 6:12 (KJV) For we wrestle not against flesh and blood, but against principalities, against powers, against the rulers of the darkness of this world, against spiritual wickedness in high places. 2 Corinthians 10:4 (KJV) (For the weapons of our warfare are not carnal, but mighty through God to the pulling down of strong holds;

Johan Weyer wrote a book called *Pseudomonarchia Daemonum*. It contained information about hours and rituals. It was written within 1583 and has a list of sixty-eight demons.

There are several classification by office mentioned in several grimoires. Grimoire describe the different host of hell and their powers such as; the three tiers from General to Officers.

In the 17th century an anonymous demonology book known as the *Lesser Key of Solomon or Lemegeton Clavivicula Salomonis* was discovered. It lists several details about unclean spirits and rituals.

Retrieved from " ^ "The Testament of Solomon", trans. F. C. Conybeare, Jewish Quarterly Review, October, 1898]

1. Conybeare, F.C. The Testament of Solomon, The Jewish Quarterly Review, Vol. 11, No. 1, (October ,1898)
2. De operatione daemonum. Tr. Marcus Collisson. Sydney 1843. Full online text, p.42-43

3. Encyclopedia of Demons and Demonology, By Rosemary Guiley, p. 28-29, Facts on File, 2009.

4. « les demons estans interrogez respondirent qu'ils estoient trois au corps de Louyse, y estans par le moyen d'vn malefice, & que le premier d'eux se nommoit Verrine, l'autre Gresil, & le dernier Sonneillon, & que tous estoient du troisiesme ordre, sçauoir au rang des Throsnes. » (Histoire admirable de la possession et conversion d'vne penitente [] exorcisee [] soubs l'authorité du R.P. F. SEBASTIEN MICHAELIS [] Edition troisiesme & derniere. Paris, Chastellain, 1614, page 3. From Michaelis's work, available on BNF: online text from Gallica Histoire admirable

5. "The Encyclopedia of Witchcraft and Demonology." Rossell Hope Robbins (1912). Bonanza Books. New York. ©1959. 1981 Edition.

6. "Barrett's The Magus at". Sacred-texts.com. Retrieved 2011-06-22.

7. A.E. Waite's "Book of Ceremonial Magic," p.97 and p.109

8. **Jump up ^** "Weyer's Pseudomonarchia Daemonum at Twilit Grotto". Esotericarchives.com. Retrieved 2011-06-22.

9. Retrieved from "http://en.wikipedia.org/wiki/Classification_of_demons (06/09/2014)

Scriptures that can be used during warfare prayers

Isaiah 54:17 No weapon that is formed against thee shall prosper; and every tongue [that] shall rise against thee in judgment thou shalt condemn. This [is] the heritage of the servants of the LORD, and their righteousness [is] of me, saith the LORD.

1 John 4:4[4]Ye are of God, little children, and have overcome them: because greater is he that is in you, than he that is in the world.

Mark 16:17-18 And these signs will follow those who believe: In My name they will cast out demons; they will speak with new tongues; [18] they will take up serpents; and if they drink anything deadly, it will by no means hurt them; they will lay hands on the sick, and they will recover."

Psalms 91:10 No evil shall befall you, Nor shall any plague come near your dwelling;

Psalms 121, Chapter 35

Place of Communion: Father God I ask you to forgive me for not yielding to your Spirit. I have not obeyed your voice neither have fully reflected your image. Give me the strength to remain focused and stable. This is the day that you have made. A new day that has never existed before and that will by no means be repeated. Help me to create a spiritual resume that will qualify me to be a conduit for your service and the right to enter into heaven. I believe that you are a God that is constantly moving, speaking, and transforming lives. I will accept your will. Receive my access and respond to redeem the time.

Life Changing Applications
1. Prayer of intercession or moderate. (Rom. 8:26, 27) Don't be afraid to recognize and confront the enemy's attacks through warfare prayer. (Matt.1:18)
2. Focus on the objective for the fast. (Est. 7:2, 3)
3. Praise God in advance. (Ps. 150)

4. Worship Time can be done in silence, by listening to music, or through reading Christian literature etc. (John 4:23, 24)
5. Reserve study time. Make an appointment and put on your schedule. (2 Tim. 2:15)
6. Create a personal confession of faith and recite it aloud to your children, your spouse, on your job, in your ministry, or to yourself. (Rom. 4:17; Heb. 11:13)
7. Meditation can be memorizing scriptures and also a time of worship. (Ps. 1:2; Josh. 1:8) Time allocated to hear a *rhema* or *logos* word from the Lord.

Chapter 6

RELEASE THE OLD TO GAIN THE NEW

*C*lutter is so easy to accumulate when we think we need everything. It is impossible to properly clean, if we are not willing to throw some things away. It may even require us to sow valuable items to those in need. We can never know what we have unless we organize and continuously purge our clothes, shoes, and food pantry etc. I would venture to say there is no room for the new, if we are not willing to let go of old stuff, baggage, or even things from the past.

Whoever Jesus sets free is free in deed. However there is a need for a constant outpour of the Holy Spirit help us overcome. Brethren, I count not myself to have apprehended: but this one thing I do, forgetting those things that are behind.

God is such an omnipresent. He is always searching for a place to dwell. However there must be a place prepared and reserved just for him. In most cases, when God blesses beyond our imagination it is difficult to let it go and start over with nothing. God is all-wise and he allows doors to close so we can believe him for the greater. He makes decision for us that we are not courageous to make for ourselves. I can remember after being married for thirteen years, we had experienced a dry spell in our marriage. God blessed me with my first salon. Things were turning around for the better and I was posed with a decision of holding on to dream that became a reality or keeping my family together by supporting my husband and his Army career. At that time I didn't understand why God would put me in this predicament. I didn't realize he was preparing me for larger territory. There was a degree of mistrust due to the brokenness I experienced during my desert season. We were able to become one again and move forward. I had to direct my attention toward the Lord like never before because I had established a successful business with loyal clientele. I searched the scriptures for a place of comfort and assurance.

"Truly I tell you," Jesus replied, "no one who has left home or brothers or sisters or mother or father or children or fields for me and the gospel [30] will fail to receive a hundred times as much in this present age: homes, brothers, sisters, mothers, children and fields—along with persecutions—and in the age to come eternal life. [31] But many who are first will be last, and the last first." (Mark 10:29-31 KJV) I wrote the date of my departure from in my Bible. Every day was a day of expectation of how this scripture would transition into my life. Three months later I got a job doing something I had never done before but I was willing see where God was leading me. I started to compare what had before with what I was currently receiving. My emotions were trying to overpower me but God was even stronger. God was still enlarging my territory and stretching my borders. I couldn't see that God was moving toward a closer relationship with him. I didn't recognize how he was ordering my steps. I just couldn't comprehend the concept of releasing old manner to receive the fresh and new. God begin to give me favor! My husband found a building; the owner waivered my deposit and curved my rent fees for several months. My husband met someone on his job that was willing to drive to Arkansas and transport my salon equipment to Oklahoma for free. I was responsible for gas.

My second salon was next to a Korean Restaurant that was very well known. Clients begin to stop in and inquire about my prices, expertise, and products. "Emmanuel's Beauty Salon" quickly gained its own advertisement. I never had a flier or business cards made for the first two years. God flexed his muscles and within two years God begin to bless me in the realm of the overflow. Another space became available next door to the place I was currently in and the salon expanded. Other stylists became interested in renting a booth from my salon. God's word had finally come to bring closure to my level of expectation at the time.

Wow! God did it five star style to me! Just when I got comfortable and all settled in, the owner of the building sold it giving us only a one week notice. I began to panic and wonder what I was going to do. We started looking for another building and God blessed once again. However, everything in it needed renovation. The ceiling tiles were stained, the carpet was not good, and the walls were in poor condition. Vernon and I tried to do as much work as possible and got professionals to finish it. We started making phone calls and, to our surprise, every person we contacted was affordable and readily available.

I shared the relocation with my employees and customers. They helped make the transition as smooth as possible. Emmanuel's was up and running for business within one week. God raised the bar of my expectation once again. God tripled the stylists in the salon. Every stylist was a blessing and we were a great team. There was a Christian atmosphere and all the clients really enjoyed their time in the salon. Vernon and I were stationed in Lawton, Oklahoma for seven years. God was conditioning me to trust him more. I believe it was important to share a portion of my testimony to give you a glimpse of how God can rearrange your life.

I didn't realize God had us in the school of Pastoral ship. We both had to make instant readjustment due to the transition of the salons. I meet a variety of people with different personalities and behaviors. We are now Pastor and Co-Pastor Johnson of the Culpepper Christian Servicemen Center. All the sacrifices we made as owners of three salons are very similar to what we are experiencing right now. I encourage you to gain all the knowledge and wisdom where you are right now because God has you in the school of personal encounter. These tactics cannot be taught. They must be experienced. We must be fully convinced that God will do a new thing and it shall spring forth if we don't stunt our growth. We don't have all the facts, details, or explanations to know that God is in control. He will make a way in the wilderness, create rivers in the desert, straighten crooked roads, and smooth rough edges.

Flexibility is essential if we going to be led by the Spirit of God, things are subject to change without warning. God see and knows the application necessary to obtain his purpose in our lives. He knows when our desert storm will force us to depend on him. In other words, he knows how to press, shape, mold, and shake into a broken and contrite heart. We have the option of looking to the hills from whence come our help, rely on our own, or be falsified by people. God knows how to perform spiritual surgery and remove things that are illegally occupying his space. Unless we are willing to let go of monumental things we will never be in the position to receive the aspects of being filled with the Holy Spirit.

Pleroo is a Greek word that means to be filled, complete in the things of God. It is a process of continuous cultivation that transforms us into the likeness of God. When we give God free reign over our finances, behavior, attitude, and interaction with others, unbelievers can see a reflection of the Holy Spirit within us. "Just as the word fullness means that which is completely filled with the presence of God and all His power, His riches, and His abundance. It is a filling to the point of overflow, complete saturation of not only His character but His abilities, His power, His authority and His agency." http://www.faithsfoundations. com/Faiths_Foundations/Word_Study_1.html © 2008 Faiths Foundations All rights reserved (Retrieved 06-09-2014)

It takes a conscious daily effort to make it a lifestyle and first nature. (Scripture) If a man therefore purges himself from these, he shall be a vessel unto honor, sanctified and fit for the master's use, and prepared unto every good work. (1 Peter 3:3, 4) Your beauty should not come from outward adornment, such as elaborate hairstyles and the wearing of gold jewelry or fine clothes. Rather, it should be that of your inner self, the unfading beauty of a gentle and quiet spirit, which is of great worth in God's sight. Humility grants us the ability to be led by the Holy Spirit. God will fill us up with the fruit of the spirit and we are able to rightfully operate in the gifts of the Spirit. The fruit of the Spirit is love, joy, peace, forbearance, kindness, goodness, faithfulness, gentleness, and self-control. Against such things there is no law. The Holy Spirit will enable us to combat the enemies: devices. *Pleroo* is an inward work with expectation of outward action formulating *pletho*.

Pletho is the outpour of *pleroo,* or the outward demonstration of the Holy Spirit manifesting miracles, signs, and wonders. According to Joel 2:28, God will pour out his Spirit on all kinds of people. Your sons and daughters will prophesy. Your elderly will have revelation from dreams; your young men will see prophetic visions. God will take complete control over the inner power and use it for a particular purpose and plan. Every container is filled from the inside out and overflows from top to bottom. The enemy knows that if people realize the power that is invested in them, how detrimental we would be to him. I encourage everyone not to live a life of mediocrity. We have the power to press in, reset, and move forward. We can outlast our problems to gain the victory every time. It is imperative to have oil in lamps so when the days of adversity arise we will be able to stand.

According to my childhood experience, I believe God approved disappointment, rejection, and isolation to prepare me for my destiny and my purpose. Although God was talking to Jeremiah, when I read this scripture I felt as if he was talking to me. Jeremiah 1:5 states: "Before I formed you in the womb I knew you, before you were born I set you apart; I appointed you as a

75

prophet to the nations." I'm influenced to believe that my father being killed in Vietnam was no surprise to God, nor was the effect it would have on me. God knew that my biological parents would not raise me. He knew that my grandmother would raise me in spite of her horrific lifestyle. He was well aware of the embarrassment I had about the house I lived in which were beneath living conditions. Nevertheless, I give God praise and contribute my childhood experience as the foundation that initiated my love and trust in God. He knows what mechanism to use to draw us to him and gear us toward totally relying on him. God blessed me to graduate from High School, which was a miracle to me.

I then became fully convinced that where I lived didn't represent the potential that was stored inside of me. When God blesses people with things they never had, it can be very difficult to let go and believe him for the greater. The concept of sowing and reaping takes faith that is nourished by expectation. People experience hardship from many things such as divorce, miscarriage, unemployment, disobedient children, and debt and health problems. God and his amazing power make all these things work for our good. We are only stewards of the blessing we are enjoying; they belong to God. God is the owner over all our possessions and he can chose to use the blessings to plant anytime, anyplace, and whomever he please. The resistance arises when we don't let God have his way and release our best for the greater.

"What do workers gain from their toil? [10] I have seen the burden God has laid on the human race. [11] He has made everything beautiful in its time. He has also set eternity in the human heart; yet no one can fathom what God has done from beginning to end. [12] I know that there is nothing better for people than to be happy and to do good while they live. [13] That each of them may eat and drink, and find satisfaction in all their toil—this is the gift of God. [14] I know that everything God does will endure forever; nothing can be added to it and nothing taken from it. God does it so that people will fear him." (Eccles. 3:9-14)

After I read this scripture immediately the thought of seed and harvest time rested on my mind. A sickle is used to gather ripe the harvest. In order for a farmer's crop to be replenished, there is a time of removing the old to gain the new. I'm simply conveying that outer layers must be removed to receive the true substance of God. Just like an onion, a banana or the shell of nuts must be removed so is our process toward maturity. I believe that is the reason for fruit planting. It places a greater demand on what's to come afterwards. It pushes our faith to action by expecting the supernatural. Whenever we are willing to first, it proves to God that is our priority and he is able to replace the substance we have rendered. I'm fully persuaded that giving tithe breaks the seal to living, walking, praying, praising, and worshipping under an open heaven. God's principles are not bias to gender, race, age, or culture. The Creator is longing to release the fullness of his power to those who will walk upright in him.

And He said, "The kingdom of God is as if a man should scatter seed on the ground, [27] and should sleep by night and rise by day, and the seed should sprout and grow, he himself does not know how. 28 For the earth yields crops by itself: first the blade, then the head, after that the full grain in the head. 29 But when the grain ripens, immediately he puts in the sickle, because the harvest has come." (Mark 4:26-29 KJV)

God has standards and levels of expectations we must meet to receive our harvest. It is necessary to endure hardship with the tenacity and motivation to overcome. Testimonies are developed and cause balance, measures, principles and conditions to be promoted. I Peter 5:10 And after you have suffered a little while, the God of all grace, who has called you to his eternal glory in Christ, will himself restore, establish, and strengthen you. Wisdom, knowledge and creativity can be discovered during times of distress, lack, and adversity. Employees work before they are given their check. They are aware of their salary, benefits, and possible incentives before the job begins. God already knows what he has invested in us. Our actions demonstrate whether we will receive all the revenue. My point is getting rid of the old sinful nature will propel us to a spiritual model of being a Christian.

Place of Communion: Lord I ask your forgiveness for holding on to things that were only meant to increase my faith and trust you more. I'm willing to release things stored in my imaginary attic and basement. Things that have hindered my healing, freedom, momentum such as pass failures, fear, frustration, doubt, unbelief, and stigmatism of me and others. God I choose to start over fresh and allow a complete overhaul of anything I have stored and things I'm carrying. I'm presenting my body a living sacrifice resenting the works of my flesh but complying with your characteristics. I can do all things through Christ that strengthens me! The best is yet come.

Life Changing Application: We sometime collect or given things that have great sentimental value to encourage or remind us of a special event. However they can sometimes become stumbling blocks and prevent us from moving forward. I provided information to assist with spring cleaning.

1. Don't be afraid to let go of the past hurts.
2. Get rid of things that have served its purpose.
3. Make space for the new and improved up-grades.
4. Oppositions can be viewed as spiritual boot camp for our destiny.
5. Ask God to deliver you from all areas of insecurities.
6. Know that God will reward, restore and replace all lost.
7. Remain in position to co-operate with God.
8. Be assured that God expect the best from us and wants us have the best.

Chapter 7

FULFILLED DESTINY

*E*veryone has a destiny to fulfill in Christ, but not everyone fulfills their destiny. We can miss our place of purpose by disobedience, making the wrong choices and a lack of persistence. We develop our destiny as we mature. However destiny is accessible through faith in God. I believe that when we really realize who we are, destiny awaits our arrival. Although God can use anything and anyone, he is depending on his children to carry out his will. Destiny is predetermined by God with a purpose for every person. We have been endowed with natural gifts, talents, and passions in our mother's womb. In order to tap into it, we must not lean to our own understanding but acknowledge God in every step we make. Destiny is fulfilled by accepting God's will for our lives.

Know who you are.

In Matthew 4:11, after fasting for forty days and forty nights, he was hungry. The tempter came to him and said, "If you are the Son of God, tell these stones to become bread." (SATAN'S TEMPTATION). Jesus answered, "It is written: 'Man shall not live on bread alone, but on every word that comes from the mouth of God.' Then the devil took him to the holy city and had him stand on the highest point of the temple. "If you are the Son of God," he said, "throw yourself down. For it is written "He will command his angels concerning you and they will lift you up in their hands, so that you will not strike your foot against a stone. Jesus answered him, "It is also written: 'Do not put the Lord your God to the test. Again, the devil took him to a very high mountain and showed him all the kingdoms of the world and their splendor. ⁹ "All this I will give you," he said, "if you will bow down and worship me. Jesus said to him, "Away from me, Satan! For it is written: 'Worship the Lord your God, and serve him only.'"

The enemy wanted to exchange food for Jesus's identity. The enemy attempted to make Jesus prove his existence. He later tried to offer him something that he already owned. He saw that Jesus was fully committed to the father and wanted the praise. Every attack of the enemy is a result of self-destruction and self- absorbing. Notice every plot was challenged to prove self-sufficient to implement pride. We will defeat the enemy just by knowing who we are. Submit to the word and watch the word to the work. In the beginning was the Word, and the Word was with God, and the Word was God. We must know that the same spirit raised Lazarus from the dead desires to reside in us. Realize the adversary contend with you in the area of your ministry to prevent you from destiny. The struggles, weaknesses, and strongholds are only fiery darts that can be quenched by the shield of faith. You maybe a parent, student, employee, or soldier, but the titles do not represent who you are in the spirit realm. It is not your final destiny.

Know your entitlements.

Destiny does not require any foundation. It only takes us knowing what has already been set in stone for us and how to get to it. In Numbers 27:4 (KJV) it shows how the daughters knew they were entitled to their father's inheritance. They knew what challenges they would face such as laws that did not favor females. The daughters of Zelophehad did factual research to plead their case before Moses. (Numbers 27:1-12 KJV) they knew who they were and were sure of their trust in God. Knowing who you are is linked to your destiny. Your destiny proves to the enemy that God gave the victory in spite of the battles. The price we must pay is within the relationship with God and be in the will. How many believers are desperate for all God has in store for us? Are you willing to be a true trooper? The wisdom of God will guide us through the mind fields of the enemy. We must keep moving forward through prayer, praise, and worship alone first and then corporally.

Get in alignment with the word of God by reflecting the image, obedience and demonstration. The enemy knows who we are and what belongs to each of us. If he can reform your image or get you to renounce who you are you will never reach destiny, receive your inheritance, reap your harvest, or enter in the Promised Land. The enemy wants to rob us of our birthrights and cut off the generational blessings already established by God. Wake up! Don't let the devil steal your entitlements! I never met my father because he was killed in Vietnam. My mother never pursued any benefits that I was entitled. I was not the beneficiary for any of his benefits. In my tenth grade year of High School, God gave me the wisdom to gain a portion of his pension. I applied those funds to obtain my cosmetology licenses. Listen, we may have felt as though we were cheated, overlooked, or neglected but God is able to restore. God has promised that no good thing will he withhold from those who trust in him. (Ps. 84:11)

Get rid of mediocrity.

Being a Christian is great but if we are not reflecting the total image of salvation we don't posses our full power and authority. There are several benefits of being adopted into the royal priesthood: it grants permissible access, authority, and responsibilities. Many of us never discover God's plan for our life until we are faced with dilemmas. Our lives are like logos—every piece can form an image. We can build confidence in God through trails, tribulations, and time! We must be mindful that everything that seems impossible. God can relinquish his power to us to press through on the victorious side. Being fulfilled is the position of satisfaction. Life may not grant everyone with the same level of possessions or realm of wealth but we have a choice of being grateful for what we may have.

Destiny is a treasure that rest in the bosom of God. His plan for our life has already been arranged and predetermined with the course of events during our journey. There is an eternal significance linked to our destiny for the kingdom's sake and generations within our lineage. We must become adamant about completing our spiritual process. Nothing else we do will matter as much as the testimonies that encourage other to keep trusting God. We may achieve educational goals, promotions on the job, or any other personal advancements but only what we do for Christ is eternal. Every attack from the enemy for righteousness causes supernatural possession. Reminisce of all the battles we experience we always learn something that will prevent us from making the same mistake over. The thought came to my mind, whose residing in my place of destiny? There are always cross-roads we must go over to get to the other side. God know the plans for our lives. He plans to prosper us and not harm us and give us an expected end. Although something or someone may be occupying our place of destiny, be willing to meet the necessary requirement. The clock is always ticking but the question is, are we redeeming the time by moving in the right direction? God expect us to live out the word of God and receive what the word of can produce.

Being pregnant is a wonderful experience. I'm not just referring to natural pregnancy but also spiritual impartations. We all know that conception must take place first. The epitome of pregnancy is giving birth. We should never become complacent because we can get pregnant because there are all types of possible complications. There should also be an obligation to that which we birth. The celebration begins after the birthing process has ended and deliverance is over. 1 Samuel 1:20 (KJV) states: So in the course of time Hannah became pregnant and gave birth to a son. She named him Samuel,[b] saying, "Because I asked the LORD for him." Even though other children were fathered by her husband Elkanah, Samuel had divine destiny and Hannah was given a double portion.

Elizabeth was barren but believed God for a son. She refused to accept her current condition to hinder destiny. God favored her faith and granted her a son name John the Baptist. Mary the mother of Jesus escaped the death decree along with the obstacle of not have a place to give birth to Jesus but God made him the Savior of the world. We should never underestimate God's surveillance on his people. He is waiting to see the intensity of our pursuit for his arrival. He performs miracles, defeats the enemy, and heals diseases just to make sure we fulfill destiny. When destiny has come full circle, it will be a magnet that will draw others into miracles, signs, and wonders, and lives will be changed forever. Accelerated thinking, expectations, confidence, and application will raise the standard of Truth in Destiny.

Process to launch Destiny

The process of being pregnant with destiny is divided into three stages. I gave natural birth to my four sons and I'm sharing my experience. The first stage begins when I started having false labor pain before the real contractions took place. Contractions are intense pain throughout duration of time. Whenever we become pregnant with kingdom appointments and assignment there will be a requirement to persevere. Be prepared for progressive changes according to our own plan so we can get in alignment with the plan of God. Our mouth is the birth canal that determines whether destiny is denied or delivered. We must continually speak faith filled words with a prophetic voice.

When delivery is taking its course there is no need for the crowd. It is at that moment in time we must push pass rejection, disappointment, worry, insecurity, sickness, all inadequacies, and things that may have been lost. God is Alpha and Omega; he has predetermined our path for purposes in exchange for our destiny.

We will all arrive on schedule according to our obedience and courage to believe beyond. Adam didn't know what was inside of him. The enemy does not want you; he wants what's inside of you. The enemy knows that your purpose will bombard his kingdom and retrieve people he has bound. Destiny will set the captive free and loose the bands of wickedness for gospel's sake. Regardless of your place in God we all have the same responsibility. The Great Commission [19] Go therefore and make disciples of all the nations, baptizing them in the name of the Father and of the Son and of the Holy Spirit, [20] teaching them to observe all things that I have commanded you; and lo, I am with you always, *even* to the end of the age." Amen.

God has promised us that if we suffer with him and the sake of righteousness, we will reign with him. He will grant us with favor and the ability to do great exploits. God is able to allow your gift to make room for you. I'm reminded of the favor granted to Joseph because there was demand for his gift. Pharaoh had a dream that tremendously frightened him, and no one could interpret his dream but Joseph. God know how to set the stage for our appearance. He will place a demand on what he has placed inside of us. Is it interesting that regardless of the challenges we face and imperfections we may have, God has put purpose inside of us that only we can fulfill. When the time came for the children of Israel to be delivered he chose Moses. He was a murderer and had a speech impediment. However his purpose was to lead the children of Israel out of Egypt and to write the Ten Commandments.

He needed Noah to rebuild a nation even though he was an alcoholic. Gideon was an obscure man from a family of no prominence but the Lord used him to defeat an enemy that was oppressive that they impoverished the people of God (Judges 6) I had many similarities, I was the first in my immediate family to graduate from high school, own my own business, and live a life totally devoted to God. Neither our childhood devastation nor our family history eliminates us from God's divine plan for our lives. God can use whomever he chooses, whenever he wants, and the purpose, at any given time.

This is the reason we should remain in a righteous position, with a pure heart, and walk in humility. God is not biased; he doesn't allow age, culture, race, past failures, or educational statuses isolate us from him. There may be more qualified, popular, or financially stable people than you but that doesn't mean that you are cut off from purpose. Began to believe in God, you and then any dream you may have. God used Josiah at the age of eight. When you think of his position in modern day terms, this would place Josiah as president! Some people would say he has no experience or who would respect him or his position? We can always debate the fact of qualifications, requirements, or customary formats but God is more concerned about obedience.

After being a salon owner of three salons for more than twenty years. I never thought I would achieve a degree nor have the opportunity to live in a foreign country. I believe God had me in training or spiritual boot camp to prepare me for ministry. Our goal should never be competitive with others, become self exalted or self absorbed. We should have the motive to show the power of faith, demonstrate the results of not giving up, and manifest God's love toward everyone. Don't despise small beginnings. Perhaps God is building godly character, sharpening your integrity, or building your faith. Often times we observe our current status and don't realize that everything begins with a seed, meaning small.

Never underestimate what's on the inside you. At this point in your life, you just may be a stay-at-home mom, getting your GED, homeless, can't seem to land your first job, or start your own business. Amos told God that he was only a herdsman and a dresser of sycamore figs but God spoke to him and to him to go prophesy to the people of Israel. (Amos 7:14-15) Avoid comparing your effectiveness toward those with titles, licenses, spiritual mentors, mega or micro but be mindful that if you are working for God to get the Glory your reward is the same. We should all be fruitful as we produce the fruit of the spirit. We should all be multiplying by leading other to Christ. We have been equipped through the word to replenish the earth and circumvent lack. God has granted us the ability to subdue the earth. Psalms 24 reminds us that the earth belongs to the Lord. If we have accepted Jesus Christ as our personal savior, we then became joint heirs with him and everything that belongs to him.

Destiny Maintained

Destiny is maintained by a life in grace. The gift of grace is charisma. Destiny is centered toward grace that is unmerited favor that can't be purchased, networked or stolen. God freely gives Grace, we can't do anything to deserve or earn it. Grace fills in the gaps of emptiness and is the mediator that connects us to operate in greatness. Grace is God given power to do his will beyond our natural ability Paul wrote in the first epistle to the Corinthian church, by the grace of God I 'am what I 'am; and His grace which was bestowed upon me was not in vain, but I labored more abundantly than they all; yet not I, but the grace of God which was with me. (1 Cor. 15:10) Paul is yet speaking to the church of today.

We are non-existent without the grace of God. I am persuaded to believe that he realized all the risk he was taking and commitments made were not for fame or fortune. It was all about not allowing the crucifixion of Jesus Christ to be in vain. Paul was the perfect example of reasonable service. The knowledge that can be gained from Paul is vital to contend with the influence of the world. We must recognize that grace is a necessary component for people to launch their horizon through their specialties to advance the kingdom of God. Destiny is sustained by humility because God resists the proud but he continuously promotes the humble.

(2 Tim. 1:9) God has saved us, and called us with a holy calling, not according to our work, but according to his own purpose and grace.

The apostle Paul mentored Timothy, He made it clear that grace and faith are both necessary to be counted in the faithful category for ministry. (1 Tim. 1:12-14) Destiny is a place of duty to share the love of God through singing, dancing, preaching, along with other gifts of the spirit. We receive salvation by grace through faith, not because we are so great or special but it is the gift of God. Faith is increased as it is exercised. The more it used the bigger it will become. Every man is given a measure of faith. Faith without action will paralyze your hope. All our righteousness is as strips of material that cannot make up a pattern without faith and the word of God. Everything we do by faith is fertilized by our confidence and the expectation of existence. The acceptance of God's plan for our life has his stamp of approval and will last throughout eternity. Know that the seed is representation of the word of God. Your seed is also your harvest it. It takes time to mature, complete phases of development, and stabilization, and to reproduce. This is what will take place in middle before Harvest Time.

Place of Communion: Today I will take a bold step to activate my faith. I'm able to pursue my position in God. Through the strength of God's character, I have experienced immense joy and have had great exploits. There will be evidence of my faith. The anointing of God came upon me to speak with authority, to sing, to break up fallow ground, and lay hands with testimonies to follow. God is giving me authority to triumph. Today is a day of great opportunity to thrust my horizon. It is happening right now because there a demand for my gift. God I receive the power to walk through doors you have opened. I will not waste time or miss the chance to make a positive difference. I am ready to be used by God, embrace the wealthy place, and walk in obedience. I have gripped on to God to accept change and unknown assistance in unfamiliar places. I believe that God will do for through me for his glory. God can turn my designs into destiny.

Life Changing Application: Everyone has the opportunity to make a lasting impression on those we meet. On the other hand, we are also given the option to fulfill our purpose in life or chose otherwise. However we must become legendary by investing in our potential. Foods for your thoughts are listed below.

1. Offer God all that we are and things we have that can be used for the kingdom of God.
2. Ask him to equip us with everything we need to fulfill his purpose with our lives.
3. Realize that excuses are only factual dilemmas that we can overcome.
4. Don't be distracted by the naysayers or what others are getting accomplished.
5. Stay focus on God's plan individually.
6. Always give God honor and take no credit for myself.
7. Keep God first and he will exceed all our expectations.
8. We will experience what it means to be successful, celebrated, enjoy divine favor, and have victory over all our inadequacies.

Chapter 8

PRAISE AND POWER

*E*veryone wants to be praised for their accomplishments. I can remember potty training my sons. They were so happy to have made it to the restroom just so they could be praised and gain confidence. They would fight over who would get the sticky from the bananas. I praised my sons for their accomplishment and that inspired them. Children want to make their parents proud. Married couples strive to be pleasing to their spouses. The excitement about achievements will promote self-esteem. We are motivated to do more and will go beyond our intent we are praised. Whenever the expectation of God is meeting in our praise, he releases power. His power enables up to fulfill his purpose. After the first few years of my marriage, I realized that praise encourages my husband to do more and it boosts his ego. Employees appreciate when their supervisor praise their hard work or resolve work complications.

Praise is a form of energy used to express, admire, commend, applaud and pay tribute for an act of worthy service. Praise is an action that shows gratitude and acknowledgement for the brilliancy of one's ability. Praise has the influence of making a person improve, elongate and invoke enthusiasm. Praise empowers, and builds self-esteem. Praise can be given to person who maybe feeling like a bottomless pit and lift them on a mountain high. Praise can turn a frown into smile. Praise can transform the mind that has been concrete to become soft as cotton. Praise has the power to change attitudes, behavior, and the intent of the heart.

Give a complement today and it will make you feel better even if you don't get a positive response. Render positive words to someone and it will make a lasting impression. (Prov. 15:23 KJV) _A man has joy in an apt answer, and how delightful is a timely word! Encouraging words reveal that someone cares about you.

It will make you feel like someone believes in you and the things you can do. Praise is the morale that will make people reach for the stars and walk on the moon!

God is not like man, he doesn't wait until we do something great to accept our praise.

He created us to praise him. He expects us to simply do what we were created to do. (Ps. 100 KJV) Let everything that has breath praise the Lord. God is basically saying, if you have life that's a reason to give me praise. There are so many ways to praise God through words, action and deeds. Living organisms have a purpose to praise God. I began to look out my window and notice the nature of God's creation. Trees are strong and standing tall with leaves that change with the seasons. Flowers are constantly blooming and used to transform the mood in the atmosphere.

The grass is green and ever changed by the time of the year. Each of the mentioned organisms praise God with reasons to up-lift, builds, and represents honor and provision. God made man in his image and the ability to rule over every living creature. Blessings were commanded upon those that are in the image of God to be fruitful, multiply and subdue the earth. (Ps. 100:4 KJV) Enter his gates with thanksgiving and his courts with praise; give thanks to him and praise his name. The gates are not just limited to a church building.

The gates consist of our home, job, gym, salon, barbershop, grocery store, mall, and every place we go. Where is the court? The outer court, the inner court, and the Holy of Holies are the courts in the Old Testament. The only way anyone could enter into those courts were through priests. Jesus Christ is now our high priest and we no longer need any other mediator. The true court to me is a place of repentance. Prayer is a place of sacrifices called the altar. (John 10:9 KJV) I am the gate; whoever enters through me will be saved. He will come in and go out, and find pasture. (Rom. 10:9 KJV) If you confess with your mouth the Lord Jesus and believe in your heart that God has raised Him from dead, you will be saved. (Ps. 119:9 KJV) Wherewithal shall a young man cleanse his way? Unless they take heed according to thy word.

There is a boomerang effect to praise. If you praise people, they tend to respond with joyous respond. God desires to live in our praise. He constantly wants to answer prayer and see dreams become reality. God is always praising us through his word. He tells us that we are the apples of his eye. We are head and not the tail. We are lenders and not the borrowers. God has described us as fearfully and wonderfully made. We are peculiar people. The word God is always, always praising us. It is the father good pleasure to bless his people God.

Unstoppable praise confirms that God is always in the midst. Our circumstance should not dictate the location of God. (Ps. 100:4 KJV) Praise can remind us of our preference and deposit perseverance for what we are expecting. There is a surge of energy exerted from human strength through praise in exchange for the power of God to enter into uncommon situations. When the power of God takes its course, the level of faith executed channels it. (Acts 16:30-31 KJV) His power is demonstrated through salvation, healing, and deliverance. The benefits of praise are a transition of the mindset, stability in our emotions, and a development of humility. Praise can reaffirm past victories and propel us for future triumphs. When we think of the penalty we deserve for wrong decisions, conversation, and actions, there is a story behind our praise. (2 Chron. 20:1-20) Praise releases emotional stress, the spirit of heaviness and breakthrough. When recognition of God's goodness is broadcast, it prompts the unbeliever's curiosity. (1 Peter 2:9-12)

When we clap our hands to praise God there are spiritual shock-waves that permeate the atmosphere. God is already in the midst. I believe that God summons his angelic host to invade problems and liberate blessings. The Hebrew word for clap is *taqa*, which mean to clatter or slap our hand together with rhythm forming an instrument. "Oh, clap your hands, all you people! Shout to God with the voice of Triumph." (Ps. 47:1) God has created weapons against the enemy through our praise. For we wrestle not against flesh and blood but principalities in high places. (Ps. 144:1)

Godly praise reestablishes the kingdom of God. Satan was an instrumental musician for praise and worship in heaven. We have been the replacement of Heaven's mass choir and instrumental orchestra. Another Hebrew word for clapping is *macha* and it mean to strike the hands together with exhilaration. The human sound of praise cannot replicate by a piano, keyboard, drums, tambourine, or any instrument used to enhance the body of Christ. However the voice can duplicate the sound of musical instruments. "He trains my hands for war, so that my arms can bend a bow of bronze." (Ps. 19:34 KJV) Our praise is the master key to unlock any form of bondage or captivity. Our power is not limited to weapons used in a physical war but more powerful in our praise to God. All musical instruments played skillfully for God invokes the presence of God and impacts the flow of the spirit.

I believe God knew that not only was Moses chosen to lead the children of Israel out of Egypt and write the Ten Commandments, but demonstrated his personal relationship with God. During that time Egypt was one of the most powerful and wealthy I believe he knew how to praise God. He had the characteristic that impressed God through his humility and reliance to trust him in spite of his fears and speech impediment. God ask Moses: "What is that in your hand?" (Exod. 4:2) I'm compelled to believe that God recognized the praise rendered to him with his hand. Although the rod or staff was the point of contact to the water, I believe the power was in Moses hand. I'm also reminded of David and his sling shot. I'm convinced that God knew David praised God while tending the sheep. Again the power was not in the smooth stone but the power that was release from his praise to defeat Goliath.

"Let the favor of the Lord our God be upon us, and establish the work of our hands upon us; yes, establish the work of our hands." (Ps. 90:17) Esther became aware of being one of the contestants for the next possible queen. I believe her praise granted her favor with the king. "And when the king saw Queen Esther standing in the court, she won favor in his sight, and he held out to Esther the golden scepter that was in his hand." (Esther 5:2) Then Esther approached the king without an invitation, which was a death sentence.

After seeing the word *scepter* it struck my attention to dig deeper. A scepter is a metal staff-like instrument that is traditionally used to represent and office of power. It is arrayed with expensive jewels and embellished patterns. The scepter is used as a seal of the king's engraved approval, authority and capital punishment. The scepter could not be sold or transferred. The only way through death of the king and down within the family linage. We all can agree that grace has taken the place of the scepter. We are no longer seeking the approval of those in authority to communicate with our Heavenly father. It doesn't matter if that encounter is through prayer, praise or worship.

Place of Communion: Lord please; accept my apology for reserving my praise. I repent for not rejoicing with those that rejoice. Forgive me for allowing my problems, oppositions, and acts of my flesh to dictate my praise. I will praise you at all times. Thank you for making me an instrument of angelic sound that is able to ambush the enemy. I realize my praise has the ability to build a hedge of protection around me. I will give compliments, encourage, and speak positive knowing that it will inspire people strive even more. I realize that my praise stabilizes my will, emotions, and spirit. Lord I thank you for equipping me with all necessary weapons to use for my benefit, but on your behalf. Lord, I thank you for rekindling my praise toward you. Today I will spark a light of flames with my voice, hands, feet, and body. Lord you created us to make a joyful sound that reflects the radiance of your glory.

Life Changing Application

Never allow our circumstances to dictate our level praise to God. We can find it easy to celebrate the blessing of God during the good times. However it is the hard phases of life, when your praise is valued the most. Remember that Satan's assignment in heaven was to praise and worship God all day and night. He gets angry when we praise God because we are his replacement. Tips listed below give reasons why we should praise God

1. Recognize that God deserves every word of encouragement, exaltation, and adoration.
2. Start the day with praising God for waking up, family, friends, and co-workers etc.
3. Be aware that we were created to praise God and our hands, feet and body are spiritual instruments.
4. See problems and oppositions as a reason to praise God.
5. Understand that praise has a boomeranged effect first on God, then yourself and those around you.
6. Realize that praise water and nurtures faith.
7. Praises towards people energizes and prompts them to do more.
8. Prayer, praise, and profession will manifest satisfying results.

Chapter 9

WORSHIP AND INTIMACY WITH GOD

*E*veryone can identify with the first person that you fell in love with. It could cause chaos if it appeared that someone or something was invading that space. I remember desiring to be the first and last person he spoke with. I was convinced that the feeling were mutual based on how I felt. I later found out that he was in love with someone else. Unlike God, he waits for those that will be consumed, focused, energized, and his feelings are always mutual. Worship is about being in love with God and the willingness to express it by any means necessary.

There are so many ways to worship God. I enjoy worshipping him by listening to soaking music because it really set the atmosphere for me to be calm, focused, and sensitive to the presence of God. I'm sure we have seen people weeping with uplifted hands, lying prostrate, or bowed down. There are several physical positions to show honor and respect. I believe a personal relationship with God and condition of the heart matters most. Worship is an individual spiritual connection with God through mediation. However worship can be done collectively but each person has their own union with God. Being in love with God is mental, emotional, and physical. Worship is internal with an outward response. I have lived in Korea for almost ten years and their custom is to bow before predominate people to show honor and respect. Being intimate with God just simply means true transparency.

The first step is to form a relationship with him by accepting him as your personal savior. Believe that there is nothing impossible with him. Nothing includes any sin you many have committed, problem that seem unbearable, or sickness that seems to be incurable. God already sees and knows everything about us. God is not an intruder, but he awaits our invitation along with our compliance to his will. Communication is how we relate and convey our thoughts and express our emotions with others. Worship is a form of communication with God from our mind, soul, and emotions. The attitude and behavior of reference to God is a matter of honesty and humility. "God is spirit, and his worshipers must worship in the Spirit and in truth." (John 4:24 KJV) The harmony of spirit and truth are a result of accepting God's love, being loved, and the ability to share love. True love can be trusted, guarantees security, and is unending. "For God so loved the world that he gave his one and only Son, that whoever believes in him shall not perish but have eternal life." (John 3:16 KJV) Every relationship depends on how deep you are willing to launch your heart.

Secondly, confess to God your deepest secrets such as strong holds, people that you have not forgiven, personal condemnations, and things that hinder your time with God. Tell God how much need and love him. During your time of worship you will develop closeness toward God. Let down your guards and allow God to permeate your heart with his Spirit. Open up the doors of your heart and invite him in to renovate the mind so you can keep it stayed on him and heart to renew a right spirit. Time invested with worship engrafts a passion to be in his presence. Private time with God through worship creates intimacy and a bond with the Holy Spirit. "He that hunger and thirst after righteousness shall be filled." (Matt. 5:6 KJV) When we become desperate for God, there is a longing to hear his voice, feel his presence, and see his manifestation.

Worship is a lifestyle of gratitude through prayer, tithing, sharing your testimony, fasting, studying the word of God, and serving others. There are no limitations to worshiping God when we have the right motives. Lastly, the essence of worship is to cultivate the nature of God internally. Worship grants us the opportunity to enter into the chambers of the king above all kings. True worship will transform, define our faith, and stabilize our relationship with God and others. You may not be the best singer but if you know how to worship, God makes melodies from your voice. You may not play an instrument like David but if you know how to worship, the presence of God will heal, deliver, and make you whole. You may not know how to preach like Paul, but if you know how to worship it will draw the lost with God's amazing grace. The church is a place to worship, but worship starts within before we get to church. Praise is a response to what God has done. Worship for who he is to you. Why not practice the applications of worship and make it a habit?

When we praise and worship God, the Glory of God falls fresh and ignites the atmosphere. Some people run, release a loud "hallelujah", or pick their feet up and put them fast. It can be perceived as dancing for the Lord. The action of praising God can be considered as spiritual fitness. We are all created to praise God but worship has requirements.

According to my knowledge, there are two words that describe the presence of God. The first word is the "anointing" which is a supernatural ability imparted by God alone and design to do a specific task.

The anointing is the mobility of God's word at work to do a specific task. In the Old Testament the priest would use virgin oil to anoint kings. Today we use the virgin oil during sacred ceremonies such as prayer, weddings, to Christian a baby, and fasting. The Greek word for anoint is *chiro* which means, "to smear or rub with oil." In 2006 I was ask to speak a Women's Conference held in Seoul Korea at the Dragon Hill Lodge. I used the illustration of peanut butter and a slice of bread as an example of what it means to smear. I took a butter knife and smeared the peanut butter on the bread. The Holy Spirit gave me the revelation that it doesn't matter how hard I tried to take the peanut butter off the bread it was impossible. Once God has anointed us to do a specific task it is not removed unless we complete it. It doesn't matter how long it takes or what we have to go through we are still anointed. When the word of God is awakened inside of us, that's when God become mobile and demonstrates his power.

My goal is to explain three levels of the word. The introduction of the trinity, God who is self-existent, Jesus is God's son conceived by God himself and the Holy Spirit given to us by the son. "In the beginning was the Word, and the Word was with God, and the Word was God." (John 1:1 KJV) Jesus was submissive to the father. "For I did not speak of my own accord, but the Father who sent me commanded me what to say and how to say it." (John 12:49 KJV) Now we are responsible to be submissive to the Holy Spirit. Keep in mind the world was created by the word of God. Jesus spoke the words of God to do his will in the life of those in the Bible that believed. Now the words we speak are directed by the condition of the heart that can be full of life or death.

Faith is the signal that connects, transport, transforms and navigates us through the dark places. Accepting, applying, and being responsible are the three levels of God's word. How much time do you really spend studying the word of God? There are many people that accept Jesus Christ as their personal savior. However they don't apply the words that he has been spoken to be the guideline or blueprint for their lives. For example, just coming to church and knowing about God is the first level. Secondly, some hear and know the word but apply the word of God in the time of trouble. Thirdly, others disregard responsibility of sharing the word and their testimony.

One of the reasons for writing this book is to challenge, propel, and motivate believers to seek the word of God. Understanding the word God and the different roles it has in Christian living is important. Realize that being obligated to the word of God and utilizing its benefits can dictate the fullness of all God has for us. The Holy Spirit, Anointing, and Glory of God are all the same. "In the beginning was the Word, and the Word was with God, and the Word was God." (John 1:2 KJV) I once believed they were different and separate from each other. I know that this information will enlighten the understanding of many.

When the word of God becomes activated with pure hands and clean hearts his presence dwells on and in that vessel. I believe that the word of God requires three "R's": response, reaction, and replication. When these three are demonstrated by faith the power of God is released at that time and in that day. "It shall come to pass in the day that his burden will be taken away from your shoulder. And his yoke from your neck. And the yoke will be destroyed because of the anointing." (Isa. 10:27 KJV)

The faith that we have in God's word with confidence and boldness becomes one with God is able to put things in alignment. "For the word of God is living and powerful and sharper than any two-edged sword, piercing even to the division of soul and spirit, and of joints and marrow, and is a discerner of the thoughts and intents of the heart." (Heb. 4:12 KJV) The responsibility of the word demonstrates the results of God's power. The word of God must have a personal effect in our lives with evidence of our spiritual encounters. Then the anointing flows from the inside out. Faith, truth and Holy Spirit combined allow us to sense his presence, hear his voice, and understand his instructions. "It is the spirit that quickeneth; the flesh profited nothing; the words that I speak unto you, they are spirit, and they are life." (John 6:63 KJV) You see the anointing is the word of God in action.

The second word is the "glory" which is the presence of God. We should acknowledge the presence God and receive and give him the liberty to be in complete control of our lives. In the Hebrew glory is known as *kabod*, which means heavy weight. (Ps. 16:11 KJV) "You make known to me the path of life; in your presence there is fullness of joy; at your right hand are pleasures forevermore." (1 John 1:1) "In the beginning was the word, and the word was with God, and the word was God."

"Who is this king of glory? The Lord strong and mighty, the Lord mighty in battle. Lift up your heads, O ye Gates; even lift them up, ye everlasting doors; and the King of glory shall come in. Who is this king of glory? The Lord of hosts, he is the king of glory. Selah." (Ps. 24:8-10 KJV) The weight of the word will presume the presence and the aroma from God that is known as the *shekinaiah* glory. The glory of God is the result of uncompromising faith that has been tried by the fire. The glory is the undeniable word exhibited from the effects of the word of God and the radiance of God himself.

Now when Solomon had finished praying, fire came down from heaven and consumed the burnt offering and the sacrifices, and the glory of the LORD FILLED THE HOUSE. [2] The priests could not enter into the house of the LORD BECAUSE THE GLORY OF THE LORD FILLED THE LORD'S HOUSE. [3] All the sons of Israel, seeing the fire come down and the glory of the LORD UPON THE HOUSE, BOWED DOWN ON THE PAVEMENT WITH THEIR FACES TO THE GROUND, AND THEY WORSHIPED AND GAVE PRAISE TO THE LORD, *saying*, "Truly He is good, truly His loving kindness is everlasting." (2 Chron. 7:7 KJV) When we have an expectation for God to show up, he will reveal his appearance with an overflow of presence that connects with the word stored in our hearts. Have you ever been in prayer with the intent of only praying for ten minutes or for a particular issue?

I have experienced the anointing taking control of my thoughts to pray for people that I never met before or a particular issue that I haven't experienced. Scriptures just begins to flow extremely fluently and the intensity of my emotions accelerates into intercession. Then, all of a sudden, although I had stop praying, I could still feel God's presence. The glory of God came and caused a stillness to take place in the room and that was the glory of God. The glory of God insures us that he is in the midst of settle our case with splendor and richness. Our level of faith, activation, and application monitors the dynamics of word of God.

The Greek word for glory is *doxazo* and it paints an image of elegance and brilliance of what the word can produce through acceptance and obedience. Solomon's kingdom is a great, conspicuous demonstration of God's word in material possessions. Keep in mind that I'm not referring to most expensive curtains, fine china, and crystal.

Solomon's father David had prepared for the presence of God. David passed the threshing floor on to be a part of the temple. The people came far and near to hear the wisdom of Solomon and to embrace the sacrifice.

Before his death, King David had provided materials in great abundance for the building of the temple on the summit of Mount Moriah. (1 Chron. 22:14, 29:4; 2 Chron. 3:1 KJV) It was there that he had purchased a threshing floor from Araunah the Jebusite on which he offered sacrifice. (2 Sam. 24:21 KJV)

According to biblical tradition, the Ark of the Covenant was solemnly brought from the tent in which David had deposited it, and into the temple, which had been prepared for its arrival. Then Solomon ascended a platform that had been erected for him, in the sight of all the people, and lifted up his hands to heaven and poured out his heart to God in prayer. (1 Kings 8:2; Chron. 6, 7 KJV) The feast of dedication, which lasted seven days, followed by the feast of tabernacles, marked a new era in the history of Israel. On the eighth day of the feast of tabernacles, Solomon dismissed the vast assemblage of the people. Wow, I can only imagine being in the presence of the threshing floor and the Ark of the Covenant.

God desires us to embrace his whole being by accepting, obeying, utilizing, and placing our absolute trust in him. "I'm the Lord and that is my name; I will not give my glory to another." (Isa. 42:8 KJV) God is simply saying that many people only want a portion of him. There are many people that don't allow the grandeur of his presence freedom. They will accept Jesus as their personal savior but have not intentions of changing their lifestyle. Some people only reverence the name of God in the time of trouble. After the storm is over he is no longer recognized. There are others who will allow being present in their services but won't allow him to move or demonstrate his power. Others treat him like a fine piece of china or fine crystal that is only used for display.

God desire us to embrace the full grandeur of his presence by accepting, obeying and utilizing the word of God through our lifestyle. "I'm the Lord that is my name; I will not give my glory to another." (Isa. 42:8) God is simply saying don't give credit to something or anyone for deeds that was only made possible through him. God deserve access to our worship, praise, in all things and at all times. When we truly worship God, the expressions of our relationship will adorn him and cause intimacy to reign supreme.

I faced major obstacles to complete my dream of writing this book. I began writing in 2005. I lost the thumb drive with all my information and did not have it save any other place, I dealt with sickness, and I overcame educational challenges and family distractions. I was extremely discouraged, condemned, and reluctant to start over. We relocated several times and I expected that it would resurface. Years had gone by and still there has been no sign of the thumb drive. I believe that I had to have personally encountered with every chapter of this book. All things work together for our good when the motive, method, and attitude are to enhance our relationship with God and enlarge the kingdom. I began to pant after God like never before. God stirred up my desire and passion to trust him to bring all things back to my remembrance. "For precept must be upon precept, precept upon precept; line upon line, line upon line; here a little, and there a little." (Isa. 28:10 KJV)

The evidence of God's power is true; I started writing again and finished this time in one year. God is able to redeem the time, if we are willing to use our time wisely. I want to encourage each person that your dream can only become reality if you make it come alive. Our goals will never be accomplished if we are not willing to pursue them. Popularity is great but if you not willing to include or promote others, how long will it last? God is searching those that will expect the greater but also willing to follow his command. (Dan. 11:32 KJV) Those who do wickedly against the covenant he shall corrupt with flattery: but the people who know their God shall be strong, and carry out great exploits. Great exploit is an opportunity, time and chance to be used by God to do thing beyond the ordinary.

God demonstrates great exploits by those who may be unqualified with disadvantages and most unlikely unknown. Great exploits are discovered through circumstances that lead us to lean and depend on God plant on a solid foundation. We receive the mysteries of God by spending time in the word of God, worship, and praise. Refuse to be comfortable, complacent, or comprise what you know to be true. There are great treasures to be discovered that reveal great exploits.

There are portals in the Holy Spirit realm that waits for those who are willing to be consistent, committed and communion with God. There are portals in the spirit realm that demand requirements to be open for example Malachi Bring ye all the tithes into the storehouse, that there may be meat in Mine house, and put Me to the proof now herewith," saith the LORD of hosts, "if I will not open to you the windows of heaven and pour you out a blessing, that there shall not be room enough to receive it.

PORTALS ARE GATEWAYS OR DOORS THAT CAN BE GOOD OR EVIL. "[10] The thief cometh not but to steal and to kill and to destroy. I am come that they might have life, and that they might have it more abundantly." (John 10:10 KJV) Our choices in life determine what we expose ourselves to. God desires us lives successful lives but there are condition we must meet. "[2] Beloved, I wish above all things that thou mayest prosper and be in health, even as thy soul prospereth." (3 John 1:2 KJV) My goal is to reach the harvest and launch more laborers in the kingdom of God. Share the dynamics of God's word. Inflate the benefits of knowing the importance of being in love with God. Expressing the need of being alone with God can enhance our relationship with him internally with him and externally with others.

Place of Communion: Father I thank you for being the perfect gentleman that operates with pure elegance and prestige. Forgive me for not loving you or totally accepting the love you have for me. I will worship you with my lifestyle opposed to just being present in a church service. Lord you are the strength of my life. Forgive me for not spending quality time with you and making you first in my life. I give you glory in the beauty of your magnificent presence just because of who you are and what you mean to me. Love is action therefore I will serve you for the rest of my life. There many adjectives I can use to describe who you are but still they do not measure the honor you deserve. Lord, thank you for the power of your word that gives me resistance, stability, and development. You are the Bishop and keeper of my mind, spirit and soul Amen. Worship emulates the sound of the shofar that is blown from heart of those seeking to please God.

Life changing application: I discovered that there are 3 level of expressing love: romance, affection, and intimacy. God could have called 12 legions to remove him from the brutal agony of pain and suffering but he endured it, just to have an intimate relationship with every person. We must make a decision and show God that his dying was not in vain.

1. I will not underestimate the power of God's word.
2. Study your word of God daily, realizing that it creates a divine connection.
3. Know that the impact of your word within me predicts and contributes to my triumph.
4. Continue to maintain my relationship with God through prayer.
5. Enlarge the family of God by witnessing to others.
6. Invest in the relationship, friendship, and fellowship of God
7. Recognize that internal sacrifices of reverence, respect, and repentance will be a result of worship.
8. Acknowledge the price of my salvation and continue to pay my debt by listening, speaking, obeying, and giving you the honor and the glory.

CLOSING REMARKS

*E*very person used by God in the Bible experienced the presence of God being alone. Mary was alone with God when an angel appeared and revealed that she would give birth to Jesus. God revealed the role of Mary to Joseph in a dream. The LORD would speak to Moses face to face the way a person speaks to a friend. Then Moses would return to the camp, but his servant, Joshua, son of Nun, a young man, did not leave the tent. Abraham was alone with God, when told that he would be the father of many nations. Noah was alone with God when instructions were given to build an Ark. After fasting for twenty-one days Daniel saw a vision of God giving him strength. When Jonah was alone in the belly of a fish, he cried out and Lord answered his prayer. Jacob was left alone with God and wrestled with an angel until his soul was blessed. Being alone with God will release miraculous benefits. When the crowd has depleted and material things can no longer be satisfying, strive to be alone with God.

CPSIA information can be obtained at www.ICGtesting.com
Printed in the USA
BVOW11s2331091114

374368BV00014B/316/P